The Synoptic Gospels

BIBLIOGRAPHIES

Tremper Longman III
General Editor and Old Testament Editor

Craig A. Evans
New Testament Editor

BIBLIOGRAPHIES No. 6

The Synoptic Gospels

An Annotated Bibliography

Scot McKnight

Matthew C. Williams

Baker Books

A Division of Baker Book House Co
Grand Rapids, Michigan 49516

Published by Baker Books
a division of Baker Book House Company
P.O. Box 6287, Grand Rapids, MI 49516-6287

Printed in the United States of America

Library of Congress Cataloging-in-Publication Data

McKnight, Scot.
    Synoptic Gospels : an annotated bibliography / Scot McKnight, Matthew C. Williams.
        p.   cm. — (IBR bibliographies ; no. 6)
    ISBN 0-8010-2227-4
    1. Bible. N.T. Gospels—Bibliography. I. Williams, Matthew C.
    II. Title. III. Series.
Z7772.M1 M35 2000
[BS2555.2]
016.226—dc21   99-055499

For information about academic books, resources for Christian leaders, and all new releases available from Baker Book House, visit our web site:
                    .   http://www.bakerbooks.com

Contents

Series Preface

With the proliferation of journals and publishing houses dedicated to biblical studies, it has become impossible for even the most dedicated scholar to keep in touch with the vast materials now available for research in all the different parts of the canon. How much more difficult for the minister, rabbi, student, or interested layperson! Herein lies the importance of bibliographies and in particular this series—IBR Bibliographies.

Bibliographies help guide students to works relevant to their research interests. They cut down the time needed to locate materials, thus providing the researcher with more time to read, assimilate, and write. These benefits are especially true for the IBR Bibliographies. First, the series is conveniently laid out along the major divisions of the canon, with four volumes planned on the Old Testament, six on the New Testament, and four on methodology. Each volume will contain approximately five hundred entries, arranged under various topics to allow for ease of reference. Since the possible entries far exceed this number, the compiler of each volume must select the more important and helpful works for inclusion. Furthermore, the entries are briefly annotated in order to inform the reader about their contents more specifically, once again giving guidance to the appropriate material and saving time by preventing the all too typical "wild goose chase" in the library.

One of the problems with published bibliographies in the past is that they are soon out of date. The development of computer-based publishing has changed this, however, and it is the plan of the Institute for Biblical Research and Baker Book House to publish updates of each volume about every five years.

Since the series is designed primarily for American and British students, the emphasis is on works written in English, with a 5 percent limit on titles not translated into English. Fortunately, a number of the most important foreign-language works have been translated into English, and wherever this is the case this information is included along with the original publication data. Again, keeping in mind the needs of the student, we have decided to list the English translation before the original title, and in this volume the titles are arranged for the most part according to the appearance of the English translation.

These bibliographies are presented under the sponsorship of the Institute for Biblical Research (IBR), an organization of evangelical Christian scholars with specialties in both Old and New Testaments and their ancillary disciplines. The IBR has met annually since 1970; its name and constitution were adopted in 1973. Besides its annual meetings (normally held the evening and morning prior to the annual meeting of the Society of Biblical Literature), the institute publishes a journal, *Bulletin for Biblical Research*, and conducts regional study groups on various biblical themes in several areas of the United States and Canada. The Institute for Biblical Research encourages and fosters scholarly research among its members, all of whom are at a level to qualify for a university lectureship. Finally, the IBR and the series editor extend their thanks to Baker Book House for its efforts to bring this series to publication. In particular, we would like to thank David Aiken for his wise guidance in giving shape to the project.

Tremper Longman III
Westmont College

Authors' Preface

A survey of recent literature, or even a brief perusal of this slender listing of items, reveals that the study of the Synoptic Gospels exceeds expectations: never has so much been said by so many in so many ways. Because the scholarship on the Synoptics has drawn its discussions from so many hermeneutical vantage points, this bibliography is organized around hermeneutical trends. Our bibliography complements the bibliography on Luke–Acts by examining each of the Synoptics.

We intend this bibliography to be useful to students and scholars alike but, if we were forced to choose between the two, we would choose the former. Consequently, we have included the items a student of the Synoptics might need to prepare a paper or to undertake some personal hunt—but we have eschewed trying to satisfy the fullness of studies needed for either doctoral studies or scholarly research. Accordingly, the user of this volume will find brief sections on textual criticism and "background" studies because these feature in good studies of the Synoptics.

In what follows, Williams has been responsible for the collection and recording of bibliographic items and for most of the annotations on the Synoptic Problem whereas McKnight is responsible for the remaining annotations. We record our debt to two of McKnight's North Park University students: Ms. Karen Wenell, who tracked down and entered into a computer so many of the annotations, and Mr. Scott Nelson, who graciously gave of his time and energy to find the items, order some through our excellent interlibrary loan system, and even suggest a few items to consider for annotations. Students like these two were uppermost in our minds in preparing the following bibliography. We also must express our appreciation to librarians who not only feast on books of this sort but who have aided our work through personal tactfulness, professional integrity, and an indefagitable commitment to make available to readers a world feasting on information. Since work for this volume took place at North Park University and Trinity Evangelical Divinity School, we wish to express our gratitude to Sonia Bodi and Keith Wells.

Scot McKnight
Matthew C. Williams

Abbreviations

AB	Anchor Bible
BETL	Bibliotheca Ephemeridum Theologicarum Lovaniensium
IBR	Institute for Biblical Research
JBL	Journal of Biblical Literature
JSP	Journal for the Study of the Pseudepigrapha
JSNT	Journal for the Study of the New Testament
JSNTSS	Journal for the Study of the New Testament, Supplement Series
NovTest	Novum Testamentum
NovTestSuppl	Novum Testamentum, Supplements
NTD	Das Neue Testament Deutsch
NTS	New Testament Studies
RevBib	Revue Biblique
SBLDS	Society of Biblical Literature, Dissertation Series
SBLMS	Society of Biblical Literature, Monograph Series
SNTSMS	Society for New Testament Studies, Monograph Series
SNTW	Studies of the New Testament and Its World
WUNT	Wissenschaftliche Untersuchungen zum Neuen Testament

1

Bibliographies, Surveys, and Introductions

The items listed in this chapter provide comprehensive bibliographies, surveys, or introductions to the basic issues in Synoptic studies.

1   B. F. Westcott. *An Introduction to the Study of the Gospels.* London: Macmillan, 1860. Eighth edition: 1895.

Old, but valuable for understanding Gospel studies at the turn of the century. Has sections on background, the origin of the Gospels, and the problems of the Gospels.

2   S. Neill and T. Wright. *The Interpretation of the New Testament, 1861–1986.* Oxford: Oxford University Press, 1964. Second edition: 1988.

Lucid, entertaining survey of the history of interpretation of the New Testament, with useful chapters on the Synoptics (pp. 112–46, 252–312, 360–449). Wright revised the book, discussing the 1961–86 period.

3   B. M. Metzger. *Index to Periodical Literature on Christ and the Gospels.* New Testament Tools and Studies 6. Leiden: E. J. Brill, 1966.

Complete listing of over 10,000 separate items about Jesus and the Gospels as found in 160 journals (in 16 languages). Arranged by both book and topic.

4   W. S. Kissinger. *The Sermon on the Mount: A History of Interpretation and Bibliography.* ATLA Bibliography Series No. 3. Lanham, Md.: Scarecrow, 1975.

A comprehensive listing of the enormous literature on the Sermon on the Mount. Now slightly dated; more recent literature has emphasized the Jewish background to Jesus' masterful Sermon.

5   D. E. Aune. *Jesus and the Synoptic Gospels: A Bibliographic Study Guide.* Theological Students Fellowship–Institute for Biblical Research Bibliographic Study Guides. Madison, Wis.: Theological Students Fellowship, 1980.
    Slightly dated; a useful guide to literature on the Synoptics, designed primarily for university students.

6   H. M. Humphrey. *A Bibliography for the Gospel of Mark 1954–1980.* Studies in the Bible and Early Christianity 1. New York: Edwin Mellen, 1981.
    A list of literature year by year. Comprehensive for the years covered.

7   G. Wagner (ed.). *An Exegetical Bibliography of the New Testament.* Volume 1: *Matthew and Mark;* Volume 2: *Luke and Acts.* Macon, Ga.: Mercer University Press, 1983, 1985.
    A tedious listing of various sorts of items by chapter and verse. Because of its approach, this work has entries that will not be found in other bibliographies.

8   D. A. Carson. *New Testament Commentary Survey.* Grand Rapids: Baker, 1986.
    Standard evangelical evaluation of commentaries. Especially helpful for expositors who need a guide for purchasing commentaries for a personal library.

9   T. R. W. Longstaff and P. A. Thomas (eds.). *The Synoptic Problem. A Bibliography, 1716–1988.* New Gospel Studies 4. Macon, Ga.: Mercer University Press, 1988.
    The most exhaustive bibliography available; designed for scholars; includes many foreign-language items.

10 F. van Segbroeck. *The Gospel of Luke: A Cumulative Bibliography 1973–1988.* BETL 88. Leuven: Leuven University Press, 1989.
    A comprehensive bibliography that contains over 2,750 entries indexed by author, subject, and Bible passage.

11 C. A. Evans. *Jesus.* IBR Bibliographies 5. Grand Rapids: Baker, 1992.
    Extremely helpful work by an expert on recent studies about Jesus. Contains material not covered by this book; especially

helpful on the most recent "lives of Jesus" and on methodologies associated with historical Jesus study. Contains helpful listings of entries concerned with noncanonical material.

12   F. Neirynck. *The Gospel of Mark: A Cumulative Bibliography
1950–1990.* BETL 102. Leuven: Leuven University Press, 1992.
Numerous entries (unnumbered) listed alphabetically, followed by complete subject indexes.

13   W. E. Mills. *The Gospel of Matthew.* Bibliographies for Biblical
Research, New Testament Series 1. Lewiston/Queenston: Edwin
Mellen, 1993.
Exhaustive bibliography of Matthew research.

14   F. W. Danker. *Multipurpose Tools for Bible Study.* St. Louis: Concordia, 1960. Revised and expanded edition: 1993.
A proven, useful tool for students who need bibliographic suggestions for doing biblical studies. Rather than simply listing
books, Danker discusses biblical studies while providing items
for further study.

15   J. B. Green and M. C. McKeever. *Luke–Acts and New Testament
Historiography.* IBR Bibliographies 8. Grand Rapids: Baker, 1994.
Complements this volume by focusing on Luke and Acts;
comprehensive and keenly aware of the current scholarship
on Luke–Acts; topics function as a guide to the recent history
of scholarship.

16   M. A. Powell. *Fortress Introduction to the Gospels.* Minneapolis: Fortress, 1997.
An excellent handbook on the Gospels; surveys introductory
matters and ten themes for each Gospel. Helpful charts.

2

Text, Language, Context, and Use of the Old Testament

Textual criticism of the Synoptics has two distinctive features: (1) the problem of assimilation and (2) the impact of the textual history for the Synoptic Problem. Every serious student of the Synoptics must learn the history of the text, for it is here that one finds the earliest commentaries on the text and one must have a text before one can interpret it.

When study of the Synoptic Gospels moves away from reconstructing the "historical Jesus," the issues of language and style immediately surface. It has long been recognized that, among the Synoptics at least, Luke measurably surpasses the others in style. However, with the growth of the literary critical approaches to the Synoptics, both Mark and Matthew have gained their admirers for their artistic ability even if their style remains pedestrian. Scholarship today is barely in its infancy when it comes to grasping the individual styles—in vocabulary, syntax, and rhetoric—of each of the Synoptists. Most grammars continue to lump the Synoptists together just as traditional studies of Jesus saw the Synoptics as one synthetic picture of Jesus. In 1981, when J. A. Fitzmyer wrote his commentary on Luke, one notes that only Nigel Turner had dared to compose a survey of Luke's style since the 1920s!

The old-fashioned expression of "background," still in use no matter how myopic it might be, has either receded in importance (for the aesthetic approaches—excepting, of course, rhetorical criticism in its culling of rhetorical parallels) or gained (because of both traditional exegesis and today's industry in historical Jesus research). A few items of special importance for the student of the Synoptic Gospels are listed, but this area knows no limits in contemporary study.

2.1 Textual Criticism

17 W. R. Farmer. *The Last Twelve Verses of Mark*. Cambridge: Cambridge University Press, 1974.

  Mark 16:9–20 is most likely original and a redactional adaptation of older traditions. Neither external nor internal criteria support the exclusion from the original text of Mark.

18 G. D. Fee. "A Text-Critical Look at the Synoptic Problem." *NovTest* 22 (1980): 12–28.

  Uses text-critical principles to discuss the Synoptic Problem; Markan priority is the best solution since it has the earliest readings most consistently; Matthew and Luke apparently had independent access to other sources, although not necessarily in written form.

19 J. K. Elliott. "L'importance de la critique textuelle pour le problem synoptique." *RevBib* 96 (1989): 56–70.

  Scholars too often use one printed Greek synopsis in studying the Synoptic Problem; wider awareness of the data is achieved by using more than one printed edition of parallels.

20 G. D. Fee. "Textual Criticism." Pp. 827–31 in *Dictionary of Jesus and the Gospels*. Edited by J. B. Green, S. McKnight, and I. H. Marshall. Downers Grove, Ill.: InterVarsity, 1992.

  Highlights the unique features of the Synoptics, including the problem of harmonization, Western "noninterpolations," and the impact, dialectically, of textual criticism on the Synoptic Problem. Textual criticism provides the primary criterion for solving the Synoptic Problem: the earlier reading is to be preferred.

21 B. D. Ehrman. *The Orthodox Corruption of Scripture: The Effect of Early Christological Controversies on the Text of the New Testament*. New York: Oxford University Press, 1993.

  Later christological controversies (e.g., adoptionism, docetism) at times influenced the texts of the Synoptics. For example, certain readings ("upon" or "into"; "as" or "as if") reveal latent Christologies in the baptismal narratives.

22   P. M. Head. "Christology and Textual Transmission: Reverential Alterations in the Synoptic Gospels." *NovTest* 35 (1993): 105–29.
Synoptic manuscripts show intentional alterations designed to protect reverence for Jesus Christ as divine; such alterations concerned names, titles, his birth, and his family but not his knowledge or his emotions.

23   K. Aland and B. Aland (eds.). *Text und Textwert der griechischen Handschriften des Neuen Testaments.* Volume IV: *Die synoptischen Evangelien.* Band 1/1–2, *Das Markusevangelium.* Arbeiten zur neutestamentlichen Textforschung 26–27. Berlin: W. de Gruyter, 1998.
The text of Mark with evaluation in light of more than two thousand ancient manuscripts.

2.2 Style and Language

24   W. K. Hobart. *The Medical Language of St. Luke.* Dublin: Hodges, Figgis, 1882. Reprinted Grand Rapids: Baker, 1954.
"The purpose of this work is to show, from an examination of the language employed in the third Gospel and the Acts of the Apostles, that both are the works of a person well acquainted with the language of the Greek Medical Schools" (p. xxix). See also Alexander, #477.

25   H. J. Cadbury. *The Style and Literary Method of Luke.* Harvard Theological Studies VI. Cambridge, Mass.: Harvard University Press, 1919–20. Reprinted New York: Kraus, 1969.
The realization that (1) each New Testament author had his own style and (2) was part of Hellenistic Greek, rather than "language of the Holy Ghost," led to this analysis of Luke's style and method. Challenges Hobart; examines Luke's use of his sources.

26   J. C. Doudna. *The Greek of the Gospel of Mark.* JBL Monograph Series 12. Philadelphia: Society of Biblical Literature and Exegesis, 1961.
Carries the work of A. Deismann to a more quantitative level; by comparing Mark to Attic Greek and the papyri, Doudna argues Mark is not "translation Greek."

27   J. H. Moulton. *A Grammar of New Testament Greek.* Volume
      IV: *Style* by N. Turner. Edinburgh: T. & T. Clark, 1976.
      Examines the Semitic and Latin backgrounds to the grammar
      of each of the Synoptists; insightful categories for the gram-
      matical and syntactical features of the Evangelists.

28   E. J. Pryke. *Redactional Style in the Marcan Gospel: A Study of
      Syntax and Vocabulary as Guides to Redaction in Mark.*
      SNTSMS 33. Cambridge: Cambridge University Press, 1978.
      An exhaustive analysis of Mark's Gospel; seeks to uncover the
      redactional elements of Mark's grammar, vocabulary, and
      style.

29   J. A. Fitzmyer. *The Gospel according to Luke: Introduction,
      Translation, and Notes.* AB 28, 28A. Garden City, N.Y.: Dou-
      bleday, 1981, 1985.
      Luke's style, grammatical improvements of Mark, vocabulary,
      Septuagintisms, and Semitisms are surveyed (1.107–127).

30   R. A. Martin. *Syntax Criticism of the Synoptic Gospels.* Studies
      in the Bible and Early Christianity 10. Lewiston/Queenston:
      Edwin Mellen, 1987.
      Develops criteria for determining Semitic sources for ancient
      documents; applies the criteria here to the Synoptics; argues
      that Matthew and Luke both used Mark; that the "Q" pas-
      sages are relatively more Semitic than Markan parallels; finds
      passages in the Synoptics that probably go back to Aramaic
      originals; the "L" material shows a high level of Semitic back-
      ground.

31   J. Engelbrecht. "The Language of the Gospel of Matthew."
      Neotestamentica 24 (1990): 199–213.
      Matthew knew Greek and Hebrew/Aramaic; his Greek is best
      classified as "synagogue Greek."

32   L. T. Stuckenbruck. "An Approach to the New Testament
      through Aramaic Sources: The Recent Methodological Debate."
      JSP 8 (1991): 3–29.
      Surveys the approach to the language of Jesus by G. Dalman,
      P. Kahle, M. Black, and J. Fitzmyer.

33   J. K. Elliott (ed.). *The Language and Style of the Gospel of Mark:
      An Edition of C. H. Turner's "Notes on Marcan Usage" together
      with Other Comparable Studies.* NovTestSuppl 71. Leiden: E. J.
      Brill, 1993.

Republication of the seminal articles of C. H. Turner on Markan style, along with essays by G. D. Kilpatrick, N. Turner, and Elliott.

34   D. L. Mealand. "Luke–Acts and the Verbs of Dionysius of Halicarnassus." *JSNT* 63 (1996): 63–86.
Luke does not consistently fit the classicizing or literary Greek style.

2.3 Contextual Studies

The Jesus traditions took shape first in the land of Israel and Galilee before moving into the broader context of diaspora Judaism. This provides the two "historical" contexts for the Synoptics. The focus here is on the material from the land of Israel ("Palestinian Judaism") but several items about the diaspora are included. It is a fact that Matthew's Gospel has been repeatedly set into its historical, social, cultural, and religious contexts but neither Mark nor Luke has had the same amount of energy devoted to their respective contexts. As with other dimensions of examining the Synoptics, frequently scholars synthesize the "context of the Synoptics," mistakenly assuming it is the same for each.

35   E. Schürer. *The History of the Jewish People in the Age of Jesus Christ (175 B.C.–A.D. 135).* Leipzig: J. C. Hinrichs, 1886. Reprinted, revised, and edited by G. Vermes, F. Millar, and M. Black. Volume 2: Edinburgh: T. & T. Clark, 1979.
The single most comprehensive study of the context of Jesus and the Gospels; examines historical context, cultural relations, political institutions, priesthood, religious parties, messianism, and the literary setting. Especially useful for those taking a historical approach to the Synoptics.

36   D. Rhoads. *Israel in Revolution: 6–74 C.E. A Political History Based on the Writings of Josephus.* Philadelphia: Fortress, 1976.
Important, politically oriented survey of the period. Highlights the role the revolutionaries played after A.D. 44. Josephus inaccurately blames one party, the Zealots; religion was important but not the only factor in the war.

37   M. Hengel. *The Zealots: Investigations into the Jewish Freedom Movement in the Period from Herod I until 70 A.D.* Translated by D. Smith. Edinburgh: T. & T. Clark, 1989. Original title: *Die*

Zeloten: Untersuchungen zur Jüdischen Freiheitsbewegung in der Zeit von Herodes I. bis 70 n. Chr. Leiden: E. J. Brill, 1961. Second edition: 1976.

Definitive treatment of the "revolutionary party" which, although rarely mentioned in the Synoptics, informs the political revolutionary theme latent in the traditions; debate over "date" of the "Zealot" party continues; the term "zeal" expresses a theological foundation, a preoccupation with Torah, a political goal, and the willingness to use violence/weapons. Eschatology shaped the movement.

38 M. Hengel. *Crucifixion: In the Ancient World and the Folly of the Message of the Cross.* Translated by J. Bowden. Philadelphia: Fortress, 1977. Original title: *"Mors turpissima crucis: Die Kreuzigung in der antiken Welt und die 'Torheit' des 'Wortes vom Kreuz,'"* in *Rechtfertigung. Festschrift für Ernst Käsemann zum 70. Geburtstag.* Edited by J. Friedrich, W. Pöhlmann, and P. Stuhlmacher. Tübingen: J. C. B. Mohr (Paul Siebeck), 1976.

Examines the social, religious, and political connotations of crucifixion at the hands of Rome; foundational for a theology of the cross.

39 H. W. Hoehner. *Herod Antipas: A Contemporary of Jesus Christ.* Cambridge: Cambridge University Press, 1972. Reprinted Grand Rapids: Zondervan, 1980.

Most complete study of Antipas in English; valuable for studying Mark 6:14–29; 8:15; 14:3–12; Luke 13:31–33.

40 J. Neusner. *The Pharisees: Rabbinic Perspectives.* Studies in Ancient Judaism I. Hoboken, N.J.: KTAV, 1973.

A detailed, form-critically, and tradition-critically based survey of the Pharisees in the rabbinic traditions; distills the author's earlier three-volume study of the Pharisees. The rabbinic traditions do not record the details of first-century Jewish life or the exact settings of their debates with Jesus.

41 J. M. Hull. *Hellenistic Magic and the Synoptic Tradition.* Studies in Biblical Theology, Second Series 28. London: SCM, 1974.

An early study of the importance of understanding Hellenistic magic to set the themes of exorcism and demons in their proper context; separate studies on Mark, Luke, and Matthew. Special emphasis is seen in Luke while Matthew has "purified" the tradition of magic. Led to later studies on Jesus by H. D. Betz, G. Twelftree, and M. Smith.

42   M. Goodman. *The Ruling Class of Judaea: The Origins of the Jewish Revolt against Rome A.D. 66–70.* Cambridge: Cambridge University Press, 1987.
Insightful analysis of the "causes" of the First Jewish Revolt against Rome (c. A.D. 66–73); special attention is given to the role of the Jewish ruling class and their decision to break off relations with Rome.

43   S. T. Lachs. *A Rabbinic Commentary on the New Testament: The Gospels of Matthew, Mark, and Luke.* Hoboken, N.J.: KTAV, 1987.
A Jewish commentary on the Synoptics by a rabbi. Helpful for providing insights into the legal and social background of Jesus.

44   S. Freyne. *Galilee, Jesus and the Gospels: Literary Approaches and Historical Investigations.* Philadelphia: Fortress, 1988.
Following his exhaustive study of Galilee (published in 1980; revised by T. & T. Clark, 1998), the author applies that study to Jesus and the Gospels: "the particularity of Jesus' Galilean career is both historically important and theologically relevant" (p. 3). Examines the social world and religious affiliations of Galilee.

45   H. Koester. *Ancient Christian Gospels: Their History and Development.* Philadelphia: Trinity Press International, 1990.
Climax to an argument sustained for decades: the canonical Gospels ought not to have privilege in reconstructing early Christian history. Studies the term "Gospel," collections of sayings, from dialogues and narrative to John, the Synoptics, and harmonizations.

46   L. I. Levine (ed.). *The Galilee in Late Antiquity.* New York/Jerusalem: The Jewish Theological Seminary of America, 1992.
Papers from the 1st International Conference on Galilean Studies in Late Antiquity at Kibbutz Hanaton (in Lower Galilee in 1989). Themes: early Christianity, aspects of society, Roman rule, rabbis and Jewry, language and literature, and archaeology.

47   E. P. Sanders. *Judaism: Practice and Belief 63 BCE–66 CE.* Philadelphia: Trinity Press International, 1992.
Responsible for the "new perspective on Paul" that led to a reformulation of how Jesus was to be seen in his context;

argues for a more responsible and positive perception of ancient Judaism. Surveys historical context and then summarizes "common Judaism" (including chapters on the temple, tithes and taxes, common theology) and the important groups and parties. Casts doubt on many Christian assumptions about Judaism and the historical integrity of the Jesus traditions when "describing" Judaism.

48   N. T. Wright. *The New Testament and the People of God.* Christian Origins and the Question of God 1. Minneapolis: Fortress, 1992.

A "story" approach to the kind of Judaism(s) that set the context for Jesus and the Synoptics; the "story" is that of God's covenant with Israel. Provides a historical basis for Wright's view that Jesus and (to different degrees) the Synoptists conceptualized their "stories" of Jesus as his ending of the exile.

49   K. E. Corley. *Private Women, Public Meals: Social Conflict in the Synoptic Tradition.* Peabody, Mass.: Hendrickson, 1993.

In the Greco-Roman world only female slaves and prostitutes would be present at public meals, with the exception of some upper-class women. Mark shows women at meals but avoids the implications; Luke upholds traditional conventions; Matthew creates an egalitarian ecclesiology. This early Christian practice is part of an "empire-wide" cultural trend.

50   R. Gray. *Prophetic Figures in Late Second Temple Jewish Palestine: The Evidence from Josephus.* New York: Oxford University Press, 1993.

Sets the context for John, Jesus, and the early Christian missionaries. Corrects the model that the prophetic office is to be defined by exclusive reference to the classical prophets; prophets had an integral relationship to prediction; some dimensions of prophecy required technical expertise (e.g., dream interpretation); connection for Josephus of prophets and priesthood.

51   F. Millar. *The Roman Near East 31 BC–AD 337.* Cambridge, Mass.: Harvard University Press, 1993.

Massive survey of the land and its people from the angle of Roman history and government; sets Israel in its geographical and chronological contexts.

52   G. H. Twelftree. *Jesus the Exorcist: A Contribution to the Study of the Historical Jesus.* Tübingen: J. C. B. Mohr (Paul Siebeck), 1993. Reprinted Peabody, Mass.: Hendrickson, 1993.

The most important study of Jesus and exorcism in the last half of the twentieth century; study of Jesus but helpful for exegesis of Synoptic references to demons and exorcisms.

53   D. R. Cartlidge, D. L. Dungan. *Documents for the Study of the Gospels.* Revised edition. Minneapolis: Fortress, 1994.
Provides "parallels" from the ancient Greek, Roman, and Jewish settings; covers the Savior, the milieu of the texts, and other "gospels."

54   R. A. Horsley. *Galilee: History, Politics, People.* Valley Forge, Pa.: Trinity Press International, 1995.
Thoroughly critical analysis of assumptions and texts; studies Galilee material especially as found in Josephus. Argues for regionalism and the autonomy from Jerusalem/Judean and its central religious orientations. Implications for studying Jesus and the Synoptics, especially in the "data bank" of evidence available, are enormous.

55   R. A. Horsely. *Archaeology, History, and Society in Galilee: The Social Context of Jesus and the Rabbis.* Valley Forge, Pa.: Trinity Press International, 1996.
Extends his previous book (#54) into Jesus, the rabbis, and their "social setting." Examines Galilee as a crossroads of empires, urbanization at Sepphoris and Tiberias, the political economy, specific villages, synagogues, and the language and cultural traditions. Methodologically broadens his base of evidence by using archaeology.

56   J. S. Kloppenborg and S. G. Wilson (eds.). *Voluntary Associations in the Graeco-Roman World.* London: Routledge, 1996.
A collection of essays mostly contributed to the Canadian Society of Biblical Studies during 1988–93. Sets synagogues, the Jesus movement, and early Christian churches in the context of ancient voluntary associations. Studies on women in ancient Jewish society are also included.

2.4 The Use of the Old Testament in the Gospels

57   B. Lindars. *New Testament Apologetic. The Doctrinal Significance of the Old Testament Quotations.* London: SCM, 1961.
Highly influential study that spawned in part a generation of examination of the use of the Old Testament in the New Tes-

tament. The church, as a result of the resurrection and its faith in Jesus' messiahship, utilized the Old Testament as was done among other Jewish movements (especially those of apocalyptic and eschatological speculation) and focused on the death of Jesus; sometimes the Old Testament text was modified.

58 R. T. France. *Jesus and the Old Testament. His Application of Old Testament Passages to Himself and His Mission.* London: Tyndale, 1971.

Studies the way Jesus used the Old Testament, with special emphasis on defining himself and his mission. Argues that the early church's use of the Old Testament stems from Jesus; invaluable excursus on Mark 13:24–27.

59 R. Longenecker. *Biblical Exegesis in the Apostolic Period.* Grand Rapids: Eerdmans, 1975.

Comprehensive survey of the use of the Old Testament in Jewish literature, Jesus (pp. 51–78), early Christian preaching, Paul, the Gospels (pp. 133–57), Hebrews, and Jewish Christian tractates. Argues that apostolic exegesis cannot be reproduced today.

60 R. T. France and D. Wenham (eds.). *Studies in Midrash and Historiography.* Gospel Perspectives 3. Sheffield: JSOT, 1983.

The rising tide of using "midrash" to explain Gospel traditions meets a breakwater; scholars include B. D. Chilton, R. Bauckham, F. F. Bruce, R. T. France, L. L. Morris, D. J. Moo, P. B. Payne, and C. L. Blomberg.

61 J. Marcus. *The Way of the Lord. Christological Exegesis of the Old Testament in the Gospel of Mark.* Louisville: Westminster/John Knox, 1992.

Investigation of Mark's Christology focusing on Christology as supported by Old Testament references; the eschatological context that responded to the destruction of Jerusalem provided Mark with an environment in which to shape his thoughts; similarities are found between Mark and Jewish exegesis.

62 C. A. Evans. "Old Testament in the Gospels." Pp. 579–90 in *Dictionary of Jesus and the Gospels.* Edited by J. B. Green, S. McKnight, and I. H. Marshall. Downers Grove, Ill.: InterVarsity, 1992.

Surveys how the Old Testament is used in each of the Synoptists along legal, prophetic, and analogical lines.

63   C. A. Evans and W. R. Stegner (eds.). *The Gospels and the Scriptures of Israel.* JSNTSS 104. Sheffield: JSOT, 1994.

   Collection of essays on how the Old Testament is used by John the Baptist, Jesus, Matthew, Mark, Luke, and John.

64   W. M. Swartley. *Israel's Scripture Traditions and the Synoptic Gospels: Story Shaping Story.* Peabody, Mass.: Hendrickson, 1994.

   An examination of how some Old Testament themes are manifested in the Evangelists: exodus/Sinai, way-conquest, temple, and kingship. Innovative approach to use of the Old Testament.

3

Methodological Issues

Gospel criticism has risen to such heights in the twentieth century that it has nearly prevented readers from seeing the Gospels themselves. Along with the rise of the historical method itself (see C. A. Evans, *Jesus* [IBR Bibliographies 5]; Grand Rapids: Baker, 1992) came the discernment of sources as well as an acceptance of the presence of "forms" that seemed to be discernible under the Gospels but which also gave indicators of the nature of primitive Christianity; following form criticism came redaction criticism, with its emphasis on the theological and social tendencies of the author and the community for whom the author speaks.

In addition to these "historical methods," a more cross-disciplinary approach has evolved and Synoptic scholars have utilized particularly the insights gained from literary-narrative-rhetorical analysis and sociological study. Each of these methods contributes to the scholarly perception of the genre of the Synoptic Gospels. This chapter will itemize important contributions to each of these disciplinary methods.

3.1 General Studies

Students often find themselves lost in a quagmire of names, movements, and schools of thought when they begin to study the Synoptic Gospels. Consequently, it is highly important that students find an introduction to the history of the various discussions about methods found in the academic circles that study the Synoptic Gospels. Many could be listed, but the following are sufficient indicators of how Gospel studies are done and will give the student a handle on names and movements.

65   J. Hastings (ed.). *A Dictionary of Christ and the Gospels.* 2 volumes. New York: Scribners, 1906–8.

An old, erudite, wordy set that covers nearly every topic imaginable (at that time). Now very dated.

66   R. Bultmann. *The History of the Synoptic Tradition.* Translated by J. Marsh. New York: Harper & Row, 1963. Revised edition: Oxford: Basil Blackwell, 1972. Reprinted Peabody, Mass.: Hendrickson, 1993. Original title: *Die Geschichte der synoptische Tradition.* Göttingen: Vandenhoeck & Ruprecht, 1921.

The influence of this book is indescribable. Bultmann discusses the various "forms" that influence how the Gospel writers went about doing their work; especially emphasizes the Greek background. Has been heavily criticized for its radical skepticism and lack of awareness of Jewish parallels and "forms." Still useful for its classification. For a detailed interaction with Bultmann, see V. Taylor, *The Gospel of Mark* (see #386).

67   N. B. Stonehouse. *The Witness of the Synoptic Gospels to Christ.* Philadelphia: The Presbyterian Guardian, 1944. Reprinted Grand Rapids: Baker, 1979.

A one-volume edition of an original two-volume edition: *The Witness of Matthew and Mark to Christ* and *The Witness of Luke to Christ.* Focuses on Christology in a balanced manner. Represents the beginning of evangelical, critical scholarship.

68   A. Farrer. *St Matthew and St Mark.* Westminster: Dacre, 1954. Second edition: 1966.

An eccentric book that seeks to explain Matthew and Mark in light of numerical codes.

69   G. E. Ladd. *The New Testament and Criticism.* Grand Rapids: Eerdmans, 1967.

Now dated; Ladd's book introduced critical methods to a generation of evangelical students in a constructive manner; provides helpful evaluations as well.

70   H. C. Kee. *Jesus in History: An Approach to the Study of the Gospels.* New York: Harcourt Brace Jovanovich, 1970. Second edition: 1977.

An introduction to the Gospels as theological treatises that interact with social and cultural conditions at the time of their writing. Includes an important chapter on the theological understanding of Q, as well as a discussion of Mark as apocalyptic history. The Gospels, from the earliest traditions on, are reflections by Christians on the event rather than historical descriptions of Jesus.

71 S. Kistemaker. *The Gospels in Current Study.* Grand Rapids: Baker, 1972.

An outdated but readable assessment of the trends in research. Contains both critical evaluation and general appreciation. Written before the rise of literary and sociological studies.

72 W. G. Kümmel. *The New Testament: The History of the Investigation of Its Problems.* Translated by S. M. Gilmour and H. C. Kee. Nashville: Abingdon, 1972. Original title: *Das Neue Testament: Geschichte der Erforschung seiner Probleme.* 1970 (second edition).

A definitive contribution to New Testament studies, with useful analyses of the historical Jesus debate as well as the history of studies on backgrounds. Its method of citing at length the publications it surveys makes the volume even more useful.

73 W. G. Kümmel. *Introduction to the New Testament.* Translated by H. C. Kee. Nashville: Abingdon, 1975. Original title: *Einleitung in das neue Testament.* Revised and updated by W. G. Kümmel; based on P. Feine and J. Behm. Seventeenth edition: Heidelburg: Quelle & Meyer, 1973.

A classic, critical presentation of the state of the art in German universities.

74 R. P. Martin. *New Testament Foundations.* Volume 1: *The Four Gospels.* Grand Rapids: Eerdmans, 1975. Second edition: 1986.

An introduction to the background of the Gospels as well as to the theological and critical issues involved in Synoptic studies. Good survey of the contours of each of the Gospels.

75 J. A. T. Robinson. *Redating the New Testament.* Berlin:de Gruyter; Westminster, 1976.

A radical departure from the status quo of dating New Testament books. Robinson contends for early dates for the Gospels; his dating of John has been intensely debated. Argues that the literature of the New Testament took shape before A.D. 70. At times this book is brilliant, if also just as often eccentric.

76   C. Brown (ed.). *History, Criticism and Faith: Four Exploratory Studies.* Leicester/Downers Grove, Ill.: InterVarsity, 1976.

Essays by G. J. Wenham, F. F. Bruce, R. T. France, and C. Brown which examine the relationship of history and faith, including an essay on the authenticity of the sayings of Jesus. Designed for university students.

77   I. H. Marshall. *New Testament Interpretation: Essays on Principles and Methods.* Exeter: Paternoster, 1977.

Alhough now slightly dated, this volume summarized several developing methods in Gospel studies. Most of these trends are now either well-known or passé; contains applications of critical methods (see the contributions of France and Martin).

78   K. F. Nickle. *The Synoptic Gospels: Conflict and Consensus.* Atlanta: John Knox, 1980.

Student introduction to the scope of the Synoptic Gospels. Now dated.

79   A. C. Thiselton. *The Two Horizons: New Testament Hermeneutics and Philosophical Description with Special Reference to Heidegger, Bultmann, Gadamer, and Wittgenstein.* Grand Rapids: Eerdmans, 1980.

Contemporary Synoptic study is applied hermeneutics. An advanced monograph on the most recent trends in modern hermeneutics. The "two horizons" are the world/intent of the author and the world/perception of the modern interpreter. See #96. Focuses on the hermeneutical issues facing Gospel scholarship with respect to the place "history" is to have in interpreting texts and the issue of referentiality.

80   H. Koester. *Introduction to the New Testament.* Volume 2: *History and Literature of Early Christianity.* Berlin: W. de Gruyter, 1982.

Introduces the reader to the New Testament according to one influential historical reconstruction of the history and growth of the early churches and their literary deposits. Koester represents the latest developments in a school of thinking that owes a great deal to Bultmann; consistently concerned with the Greco-Roman contexts of Gospel studies (in contrast to the Jewish context) and deeply indebted to more speculative reconstructions of early Christian history that are based on a thoroughgoing use of form and redaction criticism. Ignores the best of traditional scholarship.

81   P. Stuhlmacher (ed.). *The Gospel and the Gospels.* Translated by J. Bowden and J. Vriend. Grand Rapids: Eerdmans, 1991. Original title: *Das Evangelium und die Evangelien. Vorträge vom Tübinger Symposium 1982.* Tübingen: J. C. B. Mohr (Paul Siebeck), 1983.

Papers given at a symposium at Tübingen; essays on each of the Gospels as well as on both theological and critical facets of Gospel studies.

82   E. E. Ellis. "Gospels Criticism: A Perspective on the State of the Art." Pp. 26–52 in *The Gospel and the Gospels.* Grand Rapids: Eerdmans, 1991. Edited by P. Stuhlmacher. Original title: *Das Evangelium und die Evangelien. Vorträge vom Tübingen Symposium 1982.* WUNT 28. Tübingen: J. C. B. Mohr, 1983.

Masterful survey of the central issues involved in Synoptic studies; emphasizes European scholarship, especially at the turn of the century.

83   J. Dupont. *Études sur les Évangiles Synoptiques: Présentées par F. Neirynck.* 2 volumes. BETL 70 A, B. Leuven: Leuven University Press, 1985.

A massive collection of essays by France's premier Gospel scholar; essays are in French. Topics by which his essays are organized: Jesus and the origins of the Gospel traditions, the triple tradition, the double tradition, Matthew, and Luke.

84   M. A. Noll. *Between Faith and Criticism: Evangelicals, Scholarship, and the Bible in America.* SBL Confessional Perspectives Series. San Francisco: Harper & Row, 1986.

Explains how the American evangelical doctrine of Scripture accommodated itself to Gospel criticism, largely through the influence of British evangelicalism, and so overcame its fundamentalist heritage. An important read for American evangelicals.

85   C. Blomberg. *The Historical Reliability of the Gospels.* Downers Grove, Ill.: InterVarsity, 1987.

Produced in conjunction with the Tyndale House project on Gospel studies; surveys the breadth of Gospel criticism and provides an evangelical dialogue. Defends an evangelical doctrine of Scripture and history while also embracing the value of Gospel criticism.

86   S. McKnight. *Interpreting the Synoptic Gospels.* Guides to New Testament Exegesis 2. Grand Rapids: Baker, 1988.

A student's primer on the various methods used in Synoptic studies. Includes chapters on source, form, and redaction criticism, and an early critique of the then-emerging discipline of narrative/literary criticism (see #230).

87 H. C. Kee. "Synoptic Studies." Pp. 245–69 in *The New Testament and Its Modern Interpreters*. The Bible and Its Modern Interpreters. Edited by E. J. Epp and G. W. MacRae. Philadelphia: Fortress/Atlanta: Scholars, 1989.
Full survey and citation of the bibliography of recent academic scholarship, especially as found in the arenas of the Synoptic Problem and genre criticism.

88 E. P. Sanders and M. Davies. *Studying the Synoptic Gospels*. London: SCM/Philadelphia: Trinity Press International, 1989.
Student introduction to the principal issues and methods involved in studying the Synoptics.

89 G. N. Stanton. *The Gospels and Jesus*. Oxford Bible Series. Oxford: Oxford University Press, 1989.
Comprehensive guide to the basic points and debates, including chapters on each of the Gospels and methodological issues.

90 D. A. Black and D. Dockery (eds.). *New Testament Criticism and Interpretation*. Grand Rapids: Zondervan, 1991.
Seeking to update the work of Marshall (#77), this volume illustrates for students the usefulness and weaknesses of the major methods used in Synoptic studies. Contains essays by a variety of scholars on form, source, redaction, and literary criticism. Scheduled to be revised by Broadman & Holman.

91 J. B. Green, S. McKnight, and I. H. Marshall (eds.). *Dictionary of Jesus and the Gospels*. Downers Grove, Ill.: InterVarsity, 1992.
An innovative dictionary which presents a vast array of topics and issues. Up-to-date essays from a wide range of evangelical scholars on most topics facing the interpreter of the Gospels. Full bibliographies.

92 F. Van Segbroeck, et al. (eds.). *The Four Gospels: Festschrift Frans Neirynck*. BETL 100. 3 volumes. Leuven: Leuven University Press, 1992.
A massive collection of essays by many of the finest Gospel scholars in the world. An excellent example of what is going among Gospel scholars; articles are not all in English.

93 W. Baird. *History of New Testament Research*. Volume 1: *From Deism to Tübingen*. Minneapolis: Fortress, 1992.

This first volume of a projected two-volume work surveys the critical analysis of the New Testament, with careful attention to the study of the Gospels. Provides the important philosophical currents at work in the development of Synoptic methodology.

94   C. Brown. "Historical Jesus, Quest of." Pp. 326–41 in *Dictionary of Jesus and the Gospels*. Edited by J. B. Green, S. McKnight, and I. H. Marshall. Downers Grove, Ill.: InterVarsity, 1992.
Surveys the history of the discussion about the historical Jesus but in so doing highlights methodological factors at work. Brown has written a much longer study on the historical Jesus debate in Europe. See his *Jesus in European Protestant Thought, 1778–1860*. Durham, N.C.: Labyrinth, 1985. Reprinted Grand Rapids: Baker, 1988.

95   D. A. Carson, D. J. Moo, and L. Morris. *An Introduction to the New Testament*. Grand Rapids: Zondervan, 1992.
A conservative, evangelical approach to the issues surrounding New Testament studies. Helpful essays on Gospel issues.

96   A. C. Thiselton. *New Horizons in Hermeneutics*. Grand Rapids: Zondervan, 1992.
An exhaustive study on all the current trends in modern hermeneutics and hermeneutical theory. Contends that contemporary fads of subjectivism are not as legitimate as the more traditional approach of finding the author's original intention in its historical setting. Contains an exceptionally helpful chapter on feminist hermeneutics.

97   R. A. Burridge. *Four Gospels, One Jesus? A Symbolic Reading*. Grand Rapids: Eerdmans, 1994.
A brief survey of the theological uniqueness of each of the Evangelists: Mark (lion), Matthew (human face), Luke (ox), and John (eagle).

98   R. Morgan. "Which was the Fourth Gospel? The Order of the Gospels and the Unity of Scripture." *JSNT* 54 (1994): 3–28.
Suggests the Gospels should be read in "chronological" order: Mark, John, Matthew, and Luke. John responds to Mark and Luke interacts with all three.

99   M. Hengel. "Tasks of New Testament Scholarship." *Bulletin for Biblical Research* 6 (1996): 67–86. Translation of "Aufgaben der neutestamentlichen Wissenschaft." *NTS* 40 (1994): 321–57.

Critical of the trends in current New Testament scholarship; urges a return to the historical-critical method, noted by knowledge of history, primary sources, archaeology, and languages.

100 R. A. Harrisville. "A Critique of Current Biblical Criticism." *Word and World* 15 (1995): 206–13.
Examines four recent methods: new criticism, denying referentiality, oral history, and reader–response criticism. Contends that questions about what happened and historical referentiality will not disappear.

101 F. G. Downing. "Words as Deeds and Deeds as Words." *Biblical Interpretation* 3 (1995): 129–43.
The disjunction of "words" and "deeds" is inaccurate; words are in fact deeds and deeds are words.

102 C. L. Blomberg. *Jesus and the Gospels: An Introduction and Survey.* Nashville: Broadman & Holman, 1997.
Comprehensive survey of the major issues facing evangelical interpreters. Includes a survey of the life of Christ.

103 R. Bauckham (ed.). *The Gospel for All Christians: Rethinking the Gospel Audiences.* Grand Rapids: Eerdmans, 1998.
Essays by prominent United Kingdom scholars (M. B. Thompson, L. Alexander, R. A. Burridge, S. C. Barton, F. Watson) who agree that the Gospels were written for general circulation rather than for specific, putative communities. Defines "community" narrowly.

3.2 Source Criticism: Synopses and Studies

In order to study the Synoptic Problem properly, one must utilize a synopsis, of which there are several good ones. To analyze the data, it is recommended that a synopsis be underlined so that all agreements and disagreements among the Synoptists might be readily apparent. For two methods, see S. McKnight, *Interpreting the Synoptic Gospels* (Grand Rapids: Baker, 1988), pp. 40–44. If one uses the colors there recommended, one can check the underlining by comparing results with W. R. Farmer, *Synopticon* (Cambridge: Cambridge University Press, 1969). We recommend the following synopses as indispensable scholarly aids for those who desire to understand the phenomena of the Synoptics. Students who commit themselves to underlining a fair portion of a synopsis will come to terms with the phenomena themselves and, at the same time, develop a doctrine of Scripture more in keeping with the facts. Mastering the selections below, however, is no substitute for personal experience trying to resolve the Synoptic Problem.

3.2.1 Synopses

Synopses are not all alike and neither are they unquestionably "objective." Westerners read from left to right and a synopsis organized Matthew to Mark to Luke will inevitably lead to less appreciation of the Third Gospel; hence, some synopses are overtly arranged according to a theory in order to facilitate an easier grasp of its solution. It is wise to utilize several synopses for checks and balances.

104 B. de Solages. *A Greek Synopsis of the Gospels: A New Way of Solving the Synoptic Problem.* Translated by J. Baissus. Leiden: E. J. Brill/Toulouse: Institut Catholique, 1959. Original title: *Synopse grecque des Évangiles: Méthode nouvelle pour résoudre le problème synoptique.* Toulouse: Institut Catholique, 1958.

 A tabular approach to the Synoptic data, providing tables for all kinds of agreements and disagreements. Requires some effort before use will be effective.

105 H. F. D. Sparks. *A Synopsis of the Gospels: The Synoptic Gospels with the Johannine Parallels.* Philadelphia: Fortress, 1964.

 One of the few synopses that also contains John.

106 W. R. Farmer. *Synopticon: The Verbal Agreement between the Greek Texts of Matthew, Mark and Luke Contextually Exhibited.* Cambridge: Cambridge University Press, 1979.

 Provides the words of each of the Synoptics but highlights by colors the different kinds of relationships among Matthew, Mark, and Luke. An indispensable tool but harder to use because the Synoptics are not set in a parallel fashion.

107 A. Huck; revised by H. Greeven. *Synopsis of the First Three Gospels, with the Addition of the Johannine Parallels.* Tübingen: J. C. B. Mohr, 1981 (thirteenth edition) (distributed by Eerdmans in the United States). German title: *Synopse der drei ersten Evangelien, mit Beigabe der johanneischen Parallelstellen.*

 The original "Huck" (1892) was continuously reprinted and revised (by H. Lietzmann and H. G. Opitz in 1936), and then reissued with an English preface (by F. L. Cross in 1936); was the standard Synopsis until Aland (see #111). The latest editor, H. Greeven, paved an independent path with respect to the text as well by using varying column widths.

108 J. B. Orchard. *A Synopsis of the Four Gospels, in Greek, Arranged according to the Two-Gospel Hypothesis*. Macon, Ga.: Mercer University Press, 1983.

Convinced that the Aland-type of synopsis lends more credibility (and bias) to the Oxford Hypothesis, Orchard arranges his columns in the following order: Matthew, Luke, Mark (and John). This makes Mark the last one the eye meets and allows the Griesbach synthesis of Matthew and Luke to be seen in Mark's column. An important tool for the student who wishes to be exposed to more than the traditional hypothesis, although the criticism that other synopses are biased is overstated.

109 R. J. Swanson. *The Horizontal Line Synopsis of the Gospels*. Dillsboro: Western North Carolina Press, 1975. Second revised edition: Pasadena, Calif.: William Carey Library, 1984.

Innovative approach to examining the Synoptic phenomena; Swanson provides the parallels by putting them under each other rather than alongside one another. Its fragmentary nature prohibits the reader from seeing the Synoptic texts in context as well, but the approach facilitates careful comparison of expressions.

110 R. W. Funk. *New Gospel Parallels*. Volume 1: *The Synoptic Gospels*. Philadelphia: Fortress, 1985.

English synopsis by the founder and leader of the Jesus Seminar. Helpful for providing noncanonical text parallels. Probably the most complete English synopsis available.

111 K. Aland. *Synopsis Quattuor Evangeliorum*. Stuttgart: Deutsche Bibelstiftung, 1963. Fourteenth edition: 1996. In addition to this major Synopsis, the United Bible Societies has published *Synopsis of the Four Gospels* (tenth edition; New York: United Bible Societies, 1987), which provides a synopsis in English of the RSV alongside the Greek synopsis, and the exclusively English edition, *Synopsis of the Four Gospels: English Edition* (New York: United Bible Societies, 1985).

SQE is the standard synopsis because it uses the text of the standard Greek New Testament, Nestle-Aland; because it has a full apparatus; and because it appends quotations from early Christian sources that pertain to the specific text being presented. It was originally published in 1963 and has been continuously revised and improved.

112 M.-E. Boismard and A. Lamouille. *Synopsis Graeca Quattuor Evangeliorum*. Leuven/Paris: Peeters, 1986.

These two French Catholic scholars utilize an essentially Alexandrian text (but differ from Greeven [see #107] in that they frequently lean toward a Western reading), but they choose not to provide a textual apparatus for the variants. They use shorter lines for easier comparison. Each Gospel is presented continuously, and, when a Gospel pericope is found "out of order," a bold dotted line appears between the Gospels. Useful and complete.

3.2.2 Studies in the Synoptic Problem

The number of studies devoted to the Synoptic Problem is immense and no longer controllable. The following works are among the most important. For those who wish to delve further into the Synoptic Problem, the bibliography of Longstaff (see #142) is exhaustive through 1988. Besides the industry of individual scholars poring painstakingly over the data of the texts themselves, scholars of the Synoptic Problem have frequently sponsored international conferences where heated debate and constructive progress held the day. Fortunately, many of the conferences have had their papers published. A virtual history of the debate can be traced by studying such volumes. Let it be observed that one's solution to the Synoptic Problem has a decided impact on one's perception of early Christian history and the nature of the theology of each Evangelist (see Farmer, #120).

The Synoptic Problem has had several major solutions, the two most prominent being the Oxford Hypothesis (elucidated most completely in Streeter, #116) and the Griesbach Hypothesis (see Farmer, #120). French scholars, however, have moved in the direction of more hypothetical sources and a more complex history. Alongside this development, other scholars have opted for an oral history development of the Synoptics with less literary dependence (see Gerhardsson, #196). The surge of interest in narrative and literary critical approaches, not to mention the impact of neo-orthodoxy and postmodernism, has detracted from interest in the Synoptic Problem and is forming a generation of younger scholars who have not come to grip with the Synoptic Problem as a fundamentally important exegetical and historical problem. If it is the case that the Gospels are mutually interdependent (according to any number of theories), then knowledge of that relationship should have an impact on one's interpretation of a given pericope.

113 J. J. Griesbach. *Commentatio, qua Marci Evangelium totum e Matthaei et Lucae commentaris decerptum esse monstratur.* Pp. 68–135 in B. Reicke and B. Orchard (eds.). *J. J. Griesbach: Synoptic and Text-critical Studies 1776–1976.* SNTSMS 34; Cambridge: Cambridge University Press, 1978. Originally published in 1789 and revised in 1794.

The foundational statement (but cf. Henry Owen, *Observations on the Four Gospels* [London: St. Martin's, 1764]) of the so-called Griesbach Hypothesis (i.e., Matthew was used by Luke and Mark used both Matthew and Luke). The original Latin book is translated into English in this same volume (pp. 103–35).

114 J. C. Hawkins. *Horae Synopticae: Contributions to the Study of the Synoptic Problem.* Oxford: Clarendon, 1899. Second edition: 1909. Reprinted Grand Rapids: Baker, 1968. Foreword by F. F. Bruce.

Classic presentation of important data used in formulating the "Oxford Hypothesis" (see B. H. Streeter, #116).

115 W. Sanday (ed.). *Studies in the Synoptic Problem by Members of the University of Oxford.* Oxford: Clarendon, 1911.

Sanday's Seminar met from 1894 until 1910, discussing the various pericopae of the Synoptic Gospels, and forged the solution that, under the pen of B. H. Streeter (see #116), has become the dominant theory among scholars today. Because it was forged at Oxford, even though much earlier German adumbrations anticipated its full expression, it is best called the Oxford Hypothesis. Essays were written by the well-known Gospel specialists Sanday, Hawkins (see #114), Streeter (see #116), and W. C. Allen.

116 B. H. Streeter. *The Four Gospels: A Study of Origins. Treating of the Manuscript Tradition, Sources, Authorship, and Dates.* London: Macmillan, 1924.

The fundamental statement of the "Oxford Hypothesis" (Mark was first; Q was an independent source; Matthew and Luke each used both Mark and Q and then each also used a separate written source, labeled "M" and "L" respectively). Streeter's book has remained the constant reference for expounding this theory although several of his points have been significantly modified.

117 G. D. Kilpatrick. *The Origins of the Gospel according to St. Matthew.* Oxford: Oxford University Press, 1946.

Matthew was written after A.D. 90, using Mark, Q, and M, but
Matthew was designed as an exposition of the gospel in a litur-
gical context. The Gospel was also produced in debate with
Pharisaism.

118   T. W. Manson. *The Sayings of Jesus as Recorded in the Gospels
according to St. Matthew and St. Luke arranged with Introduction and Commentary.* London: SCM, 1949.
A commentary on the passages of Matthew and Luke that are
reasonably attributed to the Q source; helpful and suggestive.
Extremely influential in the history of Q studies but now has
been surpassed in technical perceptions of the theology,
nature, history, and extent of Q.

119   B. C. Butler. *The Originality of St. Matthew: A Critique of the
Two-Document Hypothesis.* Cambridge: Cambridge University
Press, 1951.
An eloquent, if at times overstated, refutation of the Oxford
Hypothesis, and a defense that Luke used Matthew and that
Mark used Matthew. Criticizes the then-reigning English
study of Streeter.

120   W. R. Farmer. *The Synoptic Problem: A Critical Analysis.* New
York: Macmillan, 1964. Reprinted with corrections, Dillsboro:
Western North Carolina Press, 1976.
A restatement of the Griesbach Hypothesis (#113) by a lead-
ing American thinker on the Synoptic Problem. As of 1988,
Farmer had over forty separate publications on the issues (see
#142, nos. 441A–464). Traces the history of discussion and
proposes a solution.

121   E. P. Sanders. *The Tendencies of the Synoptic Tradition.* SNTSMS
9. Cambridge: Cambridge University Press, 1969.
Fundamental critique of the supposed "laws of transmission"
for the development of the Jesus traditions. Influential study
of the principles that have been used to assess the supposed
age of traditions about Jesus and the priority of data used in
resolving the Synoptic Problem.

122   D. G. Buttrick. *Jesus and Man's Hope.* Volume 1. Pittsburgh:
Pittsburgh Theological Seminary, 1970.
An influential collection of essays of critical studies on the
Gospels by several influential scholars. Several studies antic-
ipated major trends that followed (X. Leon-Dufour, D. L. Dun-
gan, C. H. Talbert, J. L. Martyn).

123 D. L. Dungan. "Mark—The Abridgment of Matthew and Luke." Pp. 51–97 in *Jesus and Man's Hope*. Volume 1. Pittsburgh: Pittsburgh Theological Seminary, 1970.

Distinguished essay in defense of the Griesbach Hypothesis.

124 J. A. Fitzmyer. "The Priority of Mark and the 'Q' Source in Luke." Pp. 131–70 in *Jesus and Man's Hope*. Volume 1. Pittsburgh: Pittsburgh Theological Seminary, 1970.

Definitive study for the defense of the Oxford Hypothesis; remains the handiest survey available.

125 F. Neirynck (ed.). *The Minor Agreements of Matthew and Luke against Mark, with a Cumulative List*. BETL 37. Leuven: Leuven University Press, 1974.

An exhaustive table of the words and phrases that are common to Matthew and Luke but which disagree with Mark. These so-called minor agreements are a weakness of the Oxford Hypothesis and are here laid out for all to examine.

126 T. R. W. Longstaff. *Evidence of Conflation in Mark? A Study in the Synoptic Problem*. Missoula: Scholars, 1976.

Argues for the Griesbach Hypothesis, against the then almost completely dominant Oxford Hypothesis, by examining possible instances of conflation in Mark. The author argues that the Griesbach solution explains the phenomenon of order better than any other hypothesis in that evidence of using both Matthew and Luke is found in test cases as well as in Mark.

127 H.-H. Stoldt. *History and Criticism of the Marcan Hypothesis*. Trans. and ed. D. L. Niewyk. Introduction by W. R. Farmer. Macon, Ga.: Mercer University Press/Edinburgh: T. & T. Clark, 1980. Original title: *Geschichte und Kritik der Markushypothese*. Göttingen: Vandenhoeck & Ruprecht, 1977.

An historical critique of the priority of Mark by one who favors the Griesbach Hypothesis. Attempts to defend the Griesbach Hypothesis by illustrating the weaknesses of the so-called Oxford Hypothesis in the history of the development of that theory. Does not, however, analyze the data of the Synoptics themselves adequately.

128 J. M. Rist. *On the Independence of Matthew and Mark*. SNTSMS 32. Cambridge: Cambridge University Press, 1978.

Analyzes the middle sections of Matthew to show that Matthew and Mark may not be literarily interdependent.

129 C. M. Tuckett. "The Argument from Order and the Synoptic Problem." *Theologische Zeitschrift* 36 (1980): 338–54.

A decisive essay that rebuts the common argument used by many followers of Streeter by redefining the meaning of the phenomenon of order. A permanent piece of scholarship.

130 G. D. Fee. "A Text-Critical Look at the Synoptic Problem." *NovTest* 22 (1980): 12–28.

Uses text-critical principles to discuss the Synoptic Problem; Markan priority is the best solution since it has the earliest readings most consistently; Matthew and Luke apparently have independent access to other sources, although not necessarily in written form.

131 M. F. Lowe. "The Demise of Arguments from Order for Markan Priority." *NovTest* 24 (1982): 27–36.

The argument from order is an insufficient proof; it tends to favor the Griesbach Hypothesis.

132 W. R. Farmer. *New Synoptic Studies: The Cambridge Gospel Conference and Beyond.* Macon, Ga.: Mercer University Press, 1983.

A collection of essays from the Cambridge conference; seeks to open the minds of scholars to the possibility of the Griesbach Hypothesis.

133 C. M. Tuckett. *The Revival of the Griesbach Hypothesis: An Analysis and Appraisal.* SNTSMS 44. Cambridge: Cambridge University Press, 1983.

Brilliant survey of recent studies that seek to overturn the Oxford Hypothesis; defends, with nuance and modification, the Oxford Hypothesis.

134 I. H. Marshall. "How to Solve the Synoptic Problem: Luke 11:43 and Parallels [Matt 23:6–7, Mk 12:37–40]." Pp. 313–25 in *The New Testament Age: Essays in Honor of Bo Reicke.* Volume 2. Edited by W. C. Weinrich. Macon, Ga.: Mercer University Press, 1984.

A methodological statement with application to one piece of data; careful, minute study of individual texts is the only method for resolving the Synoptic Problem. Mark is the basis of Matthew and Luke; Matthew and Luke used independently a common source (Q).

135 C. M. Tuckett. *Synoptic Studies: The Ampleforth Conferences of 1982 and 1983.* JSNTSS 7. Sheffield: JSOT, 1984.

A collection of essays given at the international gatherings. Essays explore more than one option for resolving the Synoptic Problem.

136 A. J. Bellinzoni (ed.). *The Two-Source Hypothesis: A Critical Appraisal.* Macon, Ga.: Mercer University Press, 1985.

An important anthology of the major articles or chapters from the formative scholars on the Synoptic Problem. The editor collects essays for and against both the Oxford and Griesbach Hypotheses. An indispensable textbook.

137 B. Reicke. *The Roots of the Synoptic Gospels.* Philadelphia: Fortress, 1986.

A unique theory on the oral, and independent, and complex origins of the Synoptics.

138 B. Orchard and H. Riley. *The Order of the Synoptics. Why Three Synoptic Gospels?* Macon, Ga.: Mercer University Press, 1987.

Riley examines the phenomena involved in the argument about the order of events in the Synoptics, trying to demonstrate that Mark depends on Matthew and Luke. Orchard presents the patristic evidence pertaining to the Synoptic Problem, providing original-language texts for many hard-to-find texts. The best collection of the patristic evidence available today. Orchard then sketches a Griesbach-type of explanation for the rise of the Synoptics.

139 R. A. Martin. *Syntax Criticism of the Synoptic Gospels.* Studies in the Bible and Early Christianity 10. Lewiston/Queenston: Edwin Mellen, 1987.

Develops criteria for determining Semitic sources for ancient documents; applies the criteria here to the Synoptics; argues that Matthew and Luke both used Mark; that the "Q" passages are relatively more Semitic than Markan parallels; finds passages in the Synoptics that probably go back to Aramaic originals; the "L" material shows a high level of Semitic background.

140 D. B. Peabody. *Mark as Composer.* New Gospel Studies 1. Macon, Ga.: Mercer University Press, 1987.

Analysis of the syntax and compositional features of Mark's text by a proponent of the Griesbach Hypothesis. Highly technical.

141 R. H. Stein. *The Synoptic Problem. An Introduction.* Grand Rapids: Baker, 1987.

Student textbook for studying the Synoptic Problem. Includes chapters on form and redaction criticism.

142 T. R. W. Longstaff and P. A. Thomas. *The Synoptic Problem. A Bibliography, 1716–1988.* New Gospel Studies 4. Macon, Ga.: Mercer University Press, 1988.

An exhaustive bibliography, arranged alphabetically with an appendix listing the chronological order of the bibliography.

143 J. K. Elliott. "L'importance de la critique textuelle pour le problem synoptique." *RevBib* 96 (1989): 56–70.

Scholars too often use one printed Greek synopsis in studying the Synoptic Problem; wider awareness of the data is achieved by using more than one printed edition of parallels.

144 H. Riley. *The Making of Mark: An Exploration.* Macon, Ga.: Mercer University Press, 1989.

A commentary on Mark written from the Two-Gospel Hypothesis viewpoint to "test whether or not this process leads to a more adequate explanation of how Mark was written" (p. x). The author concludes, at the end of his commentary, that this hypothesis "stands the test" (p. 209).

145 P. Rolland. "La question synoptique demande-t-elle une reponse compliquee?" *Biblica* 70 (1989): 217–23.

Examining Mark 6:14–16 and parallels suggests a more complicated solution to the Synoptic Problem than the simple theories of the Oxford or Griesbach persuasion.

146 D. L. Dungan (ed.). *The Interrelations of the Gospels. A Symposium Led by M. É. Boismard—W. R. Farmer—F. Neirynck.* Jerusalem, 1984. Macon, Ga.: Mercer University Press, 1990.

Another collection of major papers designed to aid in the resolution of the Synoptic Problem. Leans toward the Griesbach Hypothesis but is not concerned exclusively with the Synoptic Problem.

147 S. E. Johnson. *The Griesbach Hypothesis and Redaction Criticism.* SBLMS 41. Atlanta: Scholars, 1991.

Seeks to examine the challenge of the Oxford Hypothesis that the Griesbach Hypothesis has yet to provide plausible redactional motives for its mode of operation. Surveys the shape and theology of each of the Synoptics, selects themes (reign of God, parables, Christology) and the setting of Mark. Concludes that the Oxford Hypothesis is more satisfactory at the redactional level.

148 S. McKnight. "Source Criticism." Pp. 137–72 in *New Testament Criticism and Interpretation.* Edited by D. A. Black and D. S. Dockery. Grand Rapids: Zondervan, 1991. Scheduled to be revised and reissued by Broadman & Holman.

Introduces students to the topic by surveying the recent discussion; offers support for the Oxford Hypothesis; argues that the text-critical argument is the foundational logic for a resolution. See M. C. Williams, "Is Matthew a Scribe? An Examination of the Text-Critical Argument for the Synoptic Problem." Unpublished dissertation. Trinity International University, 1996. UMI: 9631863.

149 E. Linnemann. *Is There a Synoptic Problem? Rethinking the Literary Dependence of the First Three Gospels.* Translated by R. W. Yarbrough. Grand Rapids: Baker, 1992. German edition: *Gibt es ein synoptisches Problem?* Neuhasen: Hänssler-Verlag, 1992.

Formerly a disciple of Bultmann, Linnemann was converted to a Pentecostal type of faith and her entire theological and critical outlooks were reversed. She now advocates (against nearly all of current scholarship) a view of Scripture holding that all three Synoptics arose independently and at roughly the same time. Too often overstates the evidence.

150 R. H. Stein. "Synoptic Problem." Pp. 784–92 in *Dictionary of Jesus and the Gospels.* Edited by J. B. Green, S. McKnight, and I. H. Marshall. Downers Grove, Ill.: InterVarsity, 1992.

A readable introduction to the basic positions, issues, and evidence. See #141.

151 J. Wenham. *Redating Matthew, Mark and Luke: A Fresh Assault on the Synoptic Problem.* Downers Grove, Ill.: InterVarsity, 1992.

Argues for early dates (Matthew, c. 40; Mark, c. 45; Luke, c. 54) and little literary dependence of the Synoptics on one another. Tends to agree with the early church traditions about the Synoptic Gospels. Wenham's view is a modification of Augustine's and takes more cues from patristic evidence than from the agreements and disagreements among the Synoptics.

152 D. S. New. *Old Testament Quotations in the Synoptic Gospels, and the Two-document Hypothesis.* SBL Septuagint and Cognate Studies 37. Atlanta: Scholars, 1993.

Examines the use of the Old Testament in the Synoptics to see if there is a pattern that addresses the Synoptic Problem; with respect to the appearance of the citations, the Oxford Hypothesis is preferred.

153 W. R. Farmer. *The Gospel of Jesus: The Pastoral Relevance of the Synoptic Problem.* Louisville: Westminster/John Knox, 1994.

> Summarizes a lifetime of study of the Synoptic Problem (see #120) and extends the discussion into the realm of implications for worship, theology, and ethics.

154 D. J. Neville. *Arguments from Order in Synoptic Source Criticism: A History and Critique.* New Gospel Studies 7. Macon, Ga.: Mercer University Press, 1994.

> A complete study of the history of the argument from order (both narrative sequence and order of pericopes) in the debates over the Synoptic Problem.

155 S. L. Mattila. "A Question Too Often Neglected." *NTS* 41 (1995): 199–217.

> A neglected feature of significance is how ancient writers would have used sources; suggests the Synoptists fit somewhere between those who passed on traditions and those who edited and created them; see Sanday, #115.

156 H. Ronning. "Why I Am a Member of the Jerusalem School." *Jerusalem Perspective* 48 (1995): 22–27.

> Surveys the "Jerusalem School," with names and bibliography, which argues that a Hebrew life of Jesus formed the basis of the current Gospel traditions; the most likely order of the Synoptics is Luke, Mark, and Matthew.

157 A. R. Millard. "Writing and the Gospels." *Qumran Chronicle* 5 (1995): 55–62.

> Suggests that new discoveries from Qumran illuminate our perception of how writing was done; indicates that some of Jesus' hearers may have taken notes or recorded what they heard and saw.

158 K. E. Bailey. "Middle Eastern Oral Tradition and the Synoptic Gospels." *Expository Times* 106 (1995): 363–67.

> Drawing from his extensive experience in Middle Eastern culture, the author outlines how such a culture establishes, recites, and passes on informal oral traditions; sketches the kinds of material so passed on: proverbs, riddles, poetry, parables, and stories.

159 T. L. Brodie. "Re-Opening the Quest for Proto-Luke: The Systematic Use of Judges 6–12 in Luke 16:1–18:8." *Journal of Higher Criticism* 2 (1995): 68–101.

Revives the old position of B. H. Streeter (#116). The use of the Septuagint in Judges 6–12 in this section in Luke suggests a prehistory of that section of text.

160 H. T. Fleddermann. *Mark and Q: A Study of the Overlap Texts.* BETL 122. Leuven: Leuven University Press, 1995.

Comprehensive examination of the Q texts that overlap with Mark to determine if Mark knew and used Q. Argues that Mark did know and use Q and that the differences can be explained as Markan redaction.

161 P. L. Dickerson. "The New Character Narrative in Luke–Acts and the Synoptic Problem." *JBL* 116 (1997): 291–312.

Discusses the "new character" dimension of Luke–Acts (introduction, description, story) and shows how it is more likely that Luke used Mark since neither Mark nor Matthew has such a dimension to their texts.

162 K. Paffenroth. *The Story of Jesus According to L.* JSNTSS 147. Sheffield: Sheffield Academic, 1997.

Argues for a pre-Lukan source and its probable order; the L source was significantly oral and was mostly a sayings collection; argues its place in Jewish Christianity in the middle of the first century.

163 P. M. Head. *Christology and the Synoptic Problem: An Argument for Markan Priority.* SNTSMS 94. Cambridge: Cambridge University Press, 1997.

Using the development of Christology in the Synoptics, argues that Mark is the more primitive of the three; studies various features of Christology, including specific passages, his emotions, and the worship of Jesus.

3.3 Q Studies

A continually updated bibliography on Q is by D. M. Scholer and is published annually in the *SBL Seminar Papers*. Otherwise, students can find a gateway into the world of "Q" studies by examining the bibliography of Kloppenborg's *Q Parallels* (# 171; pp. 241–46). We list here the classic studies and the more significant works of recent years.

The original proposal of Streeter (#116) has been captured in modern scholarship but has been completely reexamined. Even though only a hypothetical source, on good grounds to be sure, many today are positing and assuming stages through which the Q source passed. Each phase has its own theology and community forces giving it its shape. Although some have argued against the existence of Q (#166), Q is a solid hypothesis for explaining the similarities of Matthew and Luke even if information about its original language, nature, theology, setting, and extent is far from certain. Some historical Jesus studies are heavily dependent on Q.

164 A. Harnack. *The Sayings of Jesus. The Second Source of St. Matthew and St. Luke.* New Testament Studies 2. Translated by J. R. Wilkinson. London: Williams & Norgate/New York: G. P. Putnam's Sons, 1908. Original title: *Sprüche und Reden Jesu: Die Zweite Quelle des Matthäus und Lukas.* Beiträge zur Einleitung in das Neue Testament 2. Leipzig: J. C. Hinrichs, 1907.

> A pioneering work on Q which was the first to reconstruct the supposed Q source; includes a discussion of the value of the reconstructed source. Still of some value.

165 T. W. Manson. *The Sayings of Jesus, As Recorded in the Gospels according to St Matthew and St Luke, Arranged with Introduction and Commentary.* London: SCM, 1949. Originally published as part two of *The Mission and Message of Jesus.* Edited by H. D. A. Major, C. J. Wright, and T. W. Manson. London: SCM, 1937.

> Lucid discussion of, and commentary on, a standard (conservative) reconstruction of Q, with a useful introduction to the problems and issues. The work ends with short commentaries on the "M" and "L" material.

166 A. M. Farrer. "On Dispensing with Q." Pp. 55–88 in *Studies in the Gospels: Essays in Memory of R. H. Lightfoot.* Edited by D. E. Nineham. Oxford: Basil Blackwell, 1955.

> A decisive challenge to the Q hypothesis; argues Luke used Matthew.

167 D. Lührman. *Die Redaktion der Logienquelle.* Wissenschaftliche Monographien zum Alten und Neuen Testament 33. Neukirchen-Vluyn: Neukirchener Verlag, 1969.

> Slightly dated study of how the Q source was redacted; includes a healthy dose of speculation pertaining to Q.

168 S. Schulz. *Q—Der Spruchquelle der Evangelisten.* Zürich: Theologischer Verlag, 1972.

> Exhaustive, and highly speculative, analysis of both the supposed Q text and the (reconstructed) communities out of which it arose.

169 R. A. Edwards. *A Theology of Q: Eschatology, Prophecy, and Wisdom.* Philadelphia: Fortress, 1976.

An early, pioneering attempt to sketch the theology of the Q traditions. In some cases the lines sketched by Edwards have been filled in by subsequent scholarship.

170 J. S. Kloppenborg. *The Formation of Q: Trajectories in Ancient Wisdom Collections.* Studies in Antiquity and Christianity. Philadelphia: Fortress, 1987.

Academic analysis of the reconstructed Q source along the lines of genres and the various parallels to these genres in the ancient Greco-Roman world. Argues for the now dominant view that Q passed through three stages in its evolution. Used as the foundation for some recent studies in the historical Jesus.

171 J. S. Kloppenborg. *Q Parallels. Synopsis, Critical Notes, and Concordance.* Foundation and Facets Reference Series. Sonoma, Calif.: Polebridge, 1988.

Presentation of a reconstruction of the Q source, parallels, and translations, with an apparatus discussing the scholarly understanding of the specific Q pericope. A source book of the highest caliber.

172 F. Neirynck. *Q-Synopsis: The Double Tradition Passages in Greek.* Studiorum Novi Testamenti Auxilia 13. Leuven: Leuven University Press, 1988.

Useful, but hard to find; not as complete or helpful as Kloppenburg.

173 R. A. Piper. *Wisdom in the Q Tradition: The Aphoristic Teaching of Jesus.* SNTSMS 61. Cambridge: Cambridge University Press, 1989.

Examines how proverbs/aphorisms shaped the emerging Jesus traditions, studying aphorisms in the double tradition and outside collections. Argues there was sapiential activity behind the collections of sayings. Suggests a setting in the Hellenists behind Acts 6–7.

174 J. S. Kloppenborg, et al. *Q-Thomas Reader.* Sonoma, Calif.: Polebridge, 1990.

An introduction, translation, and brief notes to two known early Christian sayings collections; facilitates ready comparisons.

175 A. D. Jacobson. *The First Gospel: An Introduction to Q.* Foundation and Facets. Sonoma, Calif.: Polebridge, 1992.

Popular, but responsible, introduction to the issues involved in the major discussions about Q. Jacobson believes that Q needs to be read in its own context (as discerned from clues in the reconstruction of Q by the scholarly community) and not as found now in Matthew or Luke.

176 G. N. Stanton. "Q." Pp. 644–50 in *Dictionary of Jesus and the Gospels.* Edited by J. B. Green, S. McKnight, and I. H. Marshall. Downers Grove, Ill.: InterVarsity, 1992.

Introduction to the issues and evidence, with nice bibliography.

177 D. Catchpole. *The Quest for Q.* Edinburgh: T. & T. Clark, 1993.

A definitive, technical analysis of most of the Q traditions by a master of Q scholarship. Less prone than many to draw large hypotheses or to overstate what can be known about Q.

178 B. L. Mack. *The Lost Gospel: The Book of Q and Christian Origins.* San Francisco: Harper & Row, 1993.

Argues that Q reflects what his followers thought about Jesus prior to the rise of the Christian faith that emerges in the Pauline letters and the Markan Gospel. Jesus was a wandering charismatic, a Cynic-like sage, whose whole life was eventually transformed by early Christians under the category of a martyr. Canonical gospels are mythical representations of Jesus and are far removed from the more primitive Q presentation of Jesus and its community.

179 J. S. Kloppenborg (ed.). *The Shape of Q: Signal Essays on the Sayings Gospel.* Philadelphia: Fortress, 1994.

An important collection of essays on Q that deal with critical methodological issues and that, in some cases, were difficult to obtain; the studies are introduced by Kloppenborg with an essay surveying the state of the question.

180 L. E. Vaage. *Galilean Upstarts: Jesus' First Followers according to Q.* Valley Forge, Pa.: Trinity Press International, 1994.

Attempts a social sketch of the earliest followers of Jesus in Galilee on the basis of the Q traditions; concludes they were like the Cynics.

181 R. A. Piper (ed.). *The Gospel behind the Gospels: Current Studies on Q.* NovTestSuppl 75. Leiden: E. J. Brill, 1995.

The International Society of Biblical Literature meeting in Vienna in 1990 planted the seed for collecting the views of scholars and this volume records the perspectives of a variety of scholars, including R. A. Piper, C. M. Tuckett, F. Neirynck,

D. Lührmann, M. Sako, L. Vaage, R. Uro, J. M. Robinson, and J. S. Kloppenborg. An exceptional exposé of the trends in Q scholarship.

182   C. M. Tuckett. *Q and the History of Early Christianity: Studies on Q*. Peabody, Mass.: Hendrickson, 1996.
   Revised collection of essays along with new studies by the most prominent Oxford Hypothesis proponent today; includes studies on the nature of Q, John the Baptist, eschatology, Christology, wisdom, discipleship, and Israel.

183   M. D. Goulder. "Is Q a Juggernaut?" *JBL* 115 (1996): 667–81.
   Continues his challenge of the viability of the Q source by critiquing the work of C. Tuckett.

184   J. S. Kloppenborg. "The Sayings Gospel Q and the Quest for the Historical Jesus." *Harvard Theological Review* 89 (1996): 307–44.
   Argues that dependence on Q for the historical Jesus needs to be done with caution since Q, as also Mark, are the result of rhetorical and redactional purposes; Jesus is behind both.

185   E. P. Meadors. *Jesus: The Messianic Herald of Salvation*. Peabody, Mass.: Hendrickson, 1997. Originally published by Tübingen: J. C. B. Mohr, 1995.
   A robust defense of the compatibility of Q with the Markan presentation of Jesus as well as with the historical Jesus. Examines especially wisdom Christology, Jesus the Prophet, Son of Man and Kingdom, and provides a useful survey of Q studies from Schulz (#168) to Mack (#178).

186   D. C. Allison Jr. *The Jesus Tradition in Q*. Harrisburg, Pa.: Trinity Press International, 1997.
   Argues for a modification of Kloppenborg's (#170) three-stage evolution of Q and then presents (some previously published) separate studies on select Q passages.

3.4 Form Criticism

Source criticism, even before it had gained its decisive shape in the Oxford Hypothesis, was giving way in Germany to the creative impulses of form criticism, previously established by Hermann Gunkel on Old Testament studies. Gospel form critics owe their origins today to three scholars: M. Dibelius, K. L. Schmidt, and R. Bultmann, whose influence has been more lasting because he intensely classified the forms found in the Gospels. Along with their "descriptive" work, however, came "historical judgment" and it is this latter work that has been especially susceptible to criticism. Since the pioneering efforts of these, three major developments have taken place: (1) modification of Bultmann's categories (e.g., Theissen #203); (2) assessment of presuppositions, methodology, and implications (e.g., Güttgemanns, #202); and (3) a counterproposal by those who advocate a more memory-based oral development (e.g., Gerhardsson, #196).

Ultimately, form critics operate under the assumption that a given "form" is tied to a particular "setting" (i.e., worship, instruction, polemic) and that the setting is as influential in the shape and content of a given pericope as was the historical Jesus. By extension, form critics have focused their attention on the development of the early churches rather than the historical Jesus or the Synoptic Gospels.

187 M. Dibelius. *From Tradition to Gospel.* Translated by B. L. Woolf. London: Ivor Nicholson and Watson, 1934. Reprinted New York: Scribner's, 1935. Original title: *Die Formgeschichte des Evangeliums.* Tübingen: J. C. B. Mohr (Paul Siebeck), 1919. Second edition: 1933.

> An early, definitive study of the manner in which the Gospel traditions came into existence. Dibelius sees the sermon of early Christians as contributing to the growth of the Gospel traditions.

188 K. Schmidt. *Der Rahmen der Geschichte Jesu: Literarkritische Untersuchungen zur ältesten Jesusüberlieferung.* Berlin: Trowitzsch & Sohn, 1919.

> Still valuable, but unfortunately untranslated, study of the structure that the Evangelists used to organize the loosely attached Jesus traditions at their disposal. Functions as both a work of form criticism and a brief commentary on the Synoptics.

189 R. Bultmann. *The History of the Synoptic Tradition.* Translated by John Marsh. Oxford: Basil Blackwell, 1963. Reprinted New York: Harper & Row, 1976; Peabody, Mass.: Hendrickson, 1993. Original title: *Die Geschichte der synoptischen Tradition.* Forschungen zur Religion und Literatur des Alten und Neuen Testaments 12. Göttingen: Vandenhoeck & Ruprecht, 1921. Second edition: 1931. Third edition: 1957.

> The definitive study of form criticism; still rewarding for the patient student. Very skeptical and speculative; but its minute analysis is unsurpassed. Bultman was more heavily influenced

by the forms of Greek literature than Jewish but his categories remain those of modern form criticism.

190 B. S. Easton. *The Gospel before the Gospels.* New York: Charles Scribner's Sons, 1928.

An early challenge to the use of form criticism as a means of distinguishing history from myth/legend. Defends a general historically reliable orientation on the past by the Synoptists; uses what has since become known as the "criterion of dissimilarity". "It was the teaching of Jesus that produced the community and gave it its ideals, not the reverse" (p. 119).

191 E. Hoskyns and N. Davey. *The Riddle of the New Testament.* London: Faber & Faber, 1931.

The British counterpart to Easton (#190); challenges historical skepticism by arguing that the New Testament is all about witnessing to the salvific import of God's action in history through Jesus of Nazareth.

192 R. Bultmann and K. Kundsin. *Form Criticism: Two Essays on New Testament Research.* Translated by F. C. Grant. Willett, Clark, 1934. Reprinted New York: Harper Torchbooks, 1934.

Two translated essays. Bultmann's was originally a little book entitled *Die Erforschung der synoptischen Evangelien* (Giessen: A. Töpelmann, 1925; second enlarged edition: 1930), which was exhaustively elaborated in his *History of the Synoptic Tradition* (see #189).

193 V. Taylor. *The Formation of the Gospel Tradition.* London: Macmillan, 1933. Second edition: 1935.

Popular lectures introducing the English-speaking student to the form-critical studies of Bultmann and Dibelius; responsible, fairly conservative, helpful. These lectures form the basis of Taylor's magisterial commentary on Mark (#386).

194 R. O. P. Taylor. *The Groundwork of the Gospels: With Some Collected Papers.* Oxford: Basil Blackwell, 1946.

Dated; traces the origins and development of the Gospels to Peter and "other ministers," the likelihood of memorization; connects the Gospels to settings of worship and Greek forms of instruction (anticipating current concerns with "chreia"); Jesus spoke Greek and the Gospels are reliable.

195 F. C. Grant. *The Gospels: Their Origin and Their Growth.* London: Faber & Faber/New York: Harper & Brothers, 1957.

A survey of insights gaining in power that flowed from the work of B. H. Streeter (#116); extends the debate generated by Easton (#190). Proposes a theory of complex origins of the Gospels.

196 B. Gerhardsson. *Memory and Manuscript: Oral Tradition and Written Transmission in Rabbinic Judaism and Early Christianity.* Translated by E. J. Sharpe. Acta Seminarii Neotestamentici Upsaliensis 22. Lund: C. W. K. Gleerup/Copenhagen: Ejnar Munksgaard, 1961. Reprinted with #198 by Eerdmans (Grand Rapids, 1998) as one volume: *Memory and Manuscript: Oral Tradition and Written Transmission in Rabbinic Judaism and Early Christianity with Tradition and Transmission in Early Christianity*, part of the Biblical Resource series.

Brilliant analysis that sought to overturn the work of Bultmann and Dibelius; seeks to find the origins of the Gospel traditions in the Jewish method of memorization and repetition at the oral level.

197 F. W. Beare. *The Earliest Records of Jesus: A Companion to the Synopsis of the First Three Gospels.* New York: Abingdon, 1962.

Popular presentation of a more skeptical orientation to form criticism. Useful for students because of its lucid, readable format.

198 B. Gerhardsson. *Tradition and Transmission in Early Christianity.* Coniectanea Neotestamentica 20. Translated by E. J. Sharpe. Lund: C. W. K. Gleerup, 1964. Reprinted with #196 by Eerdmans (Grand Rapids, 1998) as one volume: *Memory and Manuscript: Oral Tradition and Written Transmission in Rabbinic Judaism and Early Christianity with Tradition and Transmission in Early Christianity*, part of the Biblical Resource series.

Furthers his *Memory and Manuscript* theories.

199 E. V. McKnight. *What is Form Criticism?* Guides to Biblical Scholarship New Testament Series. Philadelphia: Fortress, 1969.

A student introduction to the basic ideas of form criticism.

200 E. P. Sanders. *The Tendencies of the Synoptic Tradition.* SNTSMS 9. Cambridge: Cambridge University Press, 1969.

Fundamental critique of the supposed "laws of transmission" for the development of the Jesus traditions. Influential study of the principles that have been used to assess the supposed age of traditions about Jesus and the priority of data used in resolving the Synoptic Problem.

201 H. Riesenfeld. *The Gospel Tradition.* Translated by E. M. Rowley and R. A. Kraft. Foreword by W. D. Davies. Philadelphia: Fortress, 1970.

> English translations of Swedish, French, and German journal articles and monograph studies. Part of what has been called the "Scandinavian School"; this school emphasizes the oral nature of the origins of the Synoptics.

202 E. Güttgemanns. *Candid Questions concerning Gospel Form Criticism. A Methodological Sketch of the Fundamental Problematics of Form and Redaction Criticism.* Translation by W. G. Doty of second corrected edition. The Pittsburgh Theological Monograph Series 26. Pittsburgh: Pickwick Press, 1979. Original title: *Formgeschichte des Evangeliums: Eine methodologische Skizze der Grundlagenproblematik der Form- und Redaktionsgeschichte.* Beiträge zur evangelische Theologie, Theologische Abhandlungen 54. Munich: Chr. Kaiser Verlag, 1971.

> Crucial evaluation of the critical theories associated with German form criticism.

203 G. Theissen. *The Miracle Stories of the Early Christian Tradition.* Translated by F. McDonagh. Philadelphia: Fortress, 1983. Original title: *Urchristliche Wundergeschichten: Ein Beitrag zur formgeschichtlichen Erforschungen der synoptischen Evangelien.* Gütersloh: Mohn, 1974.

> An exhaustive cataloguing of motifs (33) and themes (6) of the miracle stories. Examination of the significance of variation of the motifs and themes and their function as symbolic actions.

204 B. Gerhardsson. *The Origins of the Gospel Tradition.* Philadelphia: Fortress, 1979. Original title: *Evangeliernas forhistoria.* Lund: Verbum-Håkan Ohlsson Forlag, 1977.

> Popular, brief presentation of the Scandinavian School.

205 W. H. Kelber. *The Oral and the Written Gospel: The Hermeneutics of Speaking and Writing in the Synoptic Tradition, Mark, Paul, and Q.* Philadelphia: Fortress, 1983.

> Jesus and the earliest movements of Christianity were oral "faiths"; Mark interrupted this "orality" with "textuality" and defeated the original orality of the faith.

206 F. Hahn. *Zur Formgeschichte des Evangeliums.* Wege der Forschung 81. Darmstadt: Wissenschaftliche Buchgesellschaft, 1985.

A collection of early, formative essays on form criticism by Dibelius, Schmidt, Bultmann, Cullmann, Hahn, Taylor, Schelkle, Albertz, and Bertram.

207 G. Theissen. *The Gospels in Context: Social and Political History in the Synoptic Tradition.* Translated by L. M. Maloney. Minneapolis: Fortress, 1991. Original title: *Lokalkolorit und Zeitgeschichte in den Evangelien.* Novum Testamentum et Orbis Antiquus 8. Göttingen: Vandenhoeck & Ruprecht, 1989.

Form-critical investigation that provides a general summary of the history of the Synoptic traditions; sees a pre-Markan Passion narrative as deriving from the 40s. Focuses on "local color" in the Jesus traditions in order to locate geographical and chronological components.

208 M. E. Boring. *The Continuing Voice of Jesus. Christian Prophecy & the Gospel Tradition.* Louisville: Westminster/John Knox, 1991.

Some of the sayings of Jesus in Q, Mark, Matthew, and Luke (John expresses Jesus in a new narrative manner) are the sayings of early Christian prophets who spoke in the name of Jesus.

209 H. Wansbrough (ed.). *Jesus and the Oral Gospel Tradition.* JSNTSS 64. Sheffield: JSOT, 1991.

Another attempt to elucidate the oral origins of the Synoptics. Signal essays by D. E. Aune, S. Talmon, P. S. Alexander, R. Riesner, B. Gerhardsson, W. Rordorf; the significance of an oral tradition is explicated by B. F. Meyer.

210 C. L. Blomberg. "Form Criticism." Pp. 243–50 in *Dictionary of Jesus and the Gospels.* Edited by J. B. Green, S. McKnight, and I. H. Marshall. Downers Grove, Ill.: InterVarsity, 1992.

An informed, incisive evaluation of form criticism; shows the connection between classic form critics and the development of the criteria of authenticity.

211 W. Kahl. *New Testament Miracle Stories in Their Religious-Historical Setting. A Religionsgeschichtliche Comparison from a Structural Perspective.* Forschungen zur Religion und Literatur des Alten und Neuen Testaments 163. Göttingen: Vandenhoeck & Ruprecht, 1994.

Combines narrative criticism, structuralism, and the history-of-religion school. Four "motifemes" in the stories: (1) initial lack, (2) preparedness, (3) performance, and (4) sanction. Jesus carries power in the situation.

3.5 Redaction Criticism

Building on the insights of the dominant Oxford Hypothesis, and in part moving away from the concern of the form critics with pre-Gospel oral traditions and the settings/churches that gave rise to such forms, early redaction critics of the 1950s and 1960s began to focus their attention on the final written record (rather than sources and preexisting forms) and how the Evangelists shaped their traditions. Further, such concerns led quite naturally into concerns with the "communities" they represented or spoke for and, consequently, the development of earliest Christianity. Debate revolved around whether redaction criticism was concerned with the distinguishable features known through redactional elements (e.g., Bornkamm, #215; Stein, #221) or through the total impact of the Gospel as a composition (Kingsbury, #368). This latter emphasis in the second generation of redaction critics quickly mutated into the development of literary/narrative criticism (Rhoads, Dewey, and Michie, #430).

212 R. H. Lightfoot. *History and Interpretation in the Gospels.* Bampton Lectures 1934. New York: Harper & Brothers, 1934.
     Interpreted and utilized the form-critical method in a positive manner in England; "history" and "theology" intermingle in the Gospels. Becomes the predecessor of redaction criticism in England through the evaluation of the Evangelists as thoroughly "theological" rather than "historical." Less skeptical than the German form critics.

213 H. Conzelmann. *The Theology of St. Luke.* Translated by G. Buswell. New York: Harper & Row/London: Faber & Faber, 1960. Original title: *Die Mitte der Zeit.* Tübingen: J. C. B. Mohr, 1953. Second edition: 1957.
     The first major redaction-critical study of Luke's theology; see #480.

214 W. Marxsen. *Mark the Evangelist. Studies on the Redaction History of the Gospel.* Translated by J. Boyce, et al. Nashville: Abingdon, 1969. Original title: *Der Evangelist Markus: Studien zur Redaktionsgeschichte des Evangeliums.* Göttingen: Vandenhoeck & Ruprecht, 1956. Second edition: 1958.
     The first major redaction-critical study of Mark's theology; see #400.

215 G. Bornkamm, G. Barth, and H. J. Held. *Tradition and Interpretation in Matthew.* Translated by P. Scott. Philadelphia: West-

minster/London: SCM, 1963. Original title: *Überleiferung und Aulegung im Matthäusevangelium.* Wissenschaftliche Monographien zum Alten und Neuen Testaments 1. Neukirchen: Neukirchener Verlag, 1960.

Attached to a seminal essay of Bornkamm are the Ph.D. theses of two of Bornkman's students (Barth, Held). While Barth's method was only slightly challenged, his conclusions have not won acceptance. Held's thesis has not met a serious rival: the miracle stories of Matthew are shaped in the direction of Christology and discipleship. Bornkamm was the first redaction critic of Matthew; see #325.

216 J. Rohde. *Rediscovering the Teachings of the Evangelists.* Translated by D. M. Barton. Philadelphia: Westminster, 1968. Original title: *Die Redaktionsgeschichtliche Methode: Einführung und Sichtung des Forschungsstandes.* Hamburg: Furche, 1966.

Thorough presentation of the views of the early (mostly German) redaction-critical studies on Matthew, Mark, and Luke. Some of these studies are otherwise nearly inaccessible.

217 N. Perrin. *What is Redaction Criticism?* Guides to Biblical Scholarship. New Testament Series. Philadelphia: Fortress, 1969.

A student's guide to both the development and contours of redaction criticism.

218 S. S. Smalley. "Redaction Criticism." Pp. 181–95 in *New Testament Interpretation. Essays on Principles and Methods.* Edited by I. H. Marshall. Exeter: Paternoster, 1977.

A nuanced analysis with an excellent grasp of the literature and its usefulness.

219 G. R. Osborne. "The Evangelical and Redaction Criticism: Critique and Methodology." *Journal of the Evangelical Theological Society* 22 (1979): 305–22.

The first challenge to, as well as appreciation of, redaction criticism by a leading evangelical scholar. His application of the method to the Great Commission led to an important discussion within evangelicalism.

220 D. A. Carson. "Redaction Criticism: On the Legitimacy and Illegitimacy of a Literary Tool." Pp. 119–42 in *Scripture and Truth.* Edited by D. A. Carson and J. D. Woodbridge. Grand Rapids: Zondervan, 1983.

A hard-hitting description and evaluation of redaction criticism and its practitioners, especially of the more radical persuasion.

221 R. H. Stein. *Gospels and Tradition: Studies on Redaction Criticism of the Synoptic Gospels.* Grand Rapids: Baker, 1991.

Republication of pioneering essays by one of the early users of redaction criticism among evangelicals. Of particular value is his essay, "What is Redaction Criticism?" where he seeks to limit redaction criticism to the analysis of the distinctive contribution of the Evangelists.

222 G. R. Osborne. "Redaction Criticism." Pp. 662–69 in *Dictionary of Jesus and the Gospels.* Edited by J. B. Green, S. McKnight, and I. H. Marshall. Downers Grove, Ill.: InterVarsity, 1992.

A balanced introduction and survey, with sensitivity to the new directions of redaction criticism.

223 P. Sellew. "Tracking the Tradition: On the Current State of Tradition-Historical Research." *Forum* 9 (1993): 217–35.

Excellent methodological study. Tradition criticism has much in its favor; problems are surveyed and the various methods used to trace the tradition's evolution.

3.6 Aesthetic Approaches

When redaction criticism evolved into composition criticism, a mild form of literary analysis of the Gospels was given a welcome: it has remained in the house of Gospel studies for two decades. Gathered here are studies of the Gospels united by the common conviction that the text must be understood as it is—before one looks at its sources, its preexisting forms, or its editor's "revisions." Such an approach involves narrative study, literary criticism, and rhetorical analysis—in short, a form of aesthetics. Contemporary Synoptic Gospel scholarship has nearly worn these approaches out but studies are continuing to be published and, among the many, the following deserve attention.

224 N. W. Lund. *Chiasmus in the New Testament. A Study in the Form and Function of Chiastic Structures.* Peabody, Mass.: Hendrickson, 1992. Original title: *Chiasmus in the New Testament. A Study in Formgeschichte.* Chapel Hill: University of North Carolina Press, 1942.

Prior to the rise of literary and narrative methods being applied to biblical studies, scholars occasionally found "literary" features in the Gospels using other methods. Lund brilliantly analyzes the presence of "chiasm," the repetition of units (from words to paragraphs) in reverse order. Lund's analysis remains a classic with enduring insights.

225 D. Rhoads and D. Michie. *Mark as Story: An Introduction to the Narrative of a Gospel.* Philadelphia: Fortress, 1982. Second edition with J. Dewey: 1999.

The first major, although brief, study from the angle of "story"; a major theorist behind this study is Seymour Chatman. See #430.

226 J. D. Kingsbury. *Matthew as Story.* Philadelphia: Fortress, 1986. Second revised and enlarged edition: 1988.

Kingsbury's earlier work was of a composition-critical nature; here he moves his understandings of Matthew into the narrative/story mode with surprisingly few changes.

227 R. C. Tannehill. *The Narrative Unity of Luke–Acts: A Literary Interpretation.* Volume 1: *The Gospel according to Luke.* Philadelphia: Fortress, 1986.

A major project on the narrative of Luke–Acts; see #463.

228 R. W. Funk. *The Poetics of Biblical Narrative.* Foundations & Facets. Literary Facets. Sonoma, Calif.: Polebridge, 1988.

Utilizing the literary theories of V. Propp, S. Chatman, G. Genett, and S. Rimmon-Kenan, a "poetics of story" is developed to show how the various elements (events) have been connected into a whole (story). Advances through use of more than one literary theorist.

229 W. A. Kort. *Story, Text, and Scripture: Literary Interests in Biblical Narrative.* University Park: Pennsylvania State University Press, 1988.

Wide-ranging study of the kind of view of Scripture one has when one has a literary concept and approach to the narratives of Scripture. Forceful presentation.

230 S. McKnight. "Literary Criticism." Pp. 121–37 in *Interpreting the Synoptic Gospels.* Guides to New Testament Exegesis 2. Grand Rapids: Baker, 1988.

An early evaluation of the methods connected with literary and narrative approaches to the Gospels. Argues that the classic tradition-critical and historical approaches can be augmented with the literary but cannot be replaced by them.

231 B. L. Mack and V. K. Robbins. *Patterns of Persuasion in the Gospels.* Foundations & Facets. Literary Facets. Sonoma, Calif.: Polebridge, 1989.

An examination of various passages and chreia in light of rhetorical theory and practice common in the Hellenistic culture.

232 S. D. Moore. *Literary Criticism and the Gospels: The Theoretical Challenge.* New Haven: Yale University Press, 1989.
Examines recent work on the Gospels that uses narrative and reader–response criticism as well as poststructuralism. Challenges the pillars of how biblical studies have been done and can be done in light of deconstruction theory.

233 B. L. Mack. *Rhetoric and the New Testament.* Guides to Biblical Scholarship. New Testament Series. Minneapolis: Fortress, 1990.
A useful student guide to rhetorical criticism; presents the rise of the field and its context in classical rhetoric.

234 R. M. Fowler. *Let the Reader Understand: Reader–Response Criticism and the Gospel of Mark.* Minneapolis: Fortress, 1991.
Hoping to dismantle and deconstruct the New Testament guild of its preoccupation with author's intention and original sense; focus is on what the text does to its readers through its own rhetoric.

235 A. N. Wilder. *The Bible and the Literary Critic.* Minneapolis: Fortress, 1991.
Collection of (most previously published) essays grouped in three categories: new soundings; reminiscences of a changing discipline; and genres, rhetoric, and meanings.

236 J. C. Anderson and S. D. Moore (eds.). *Mark and Method: New Approaches in Biblical Studies.* Minneapolis: Fortress, 1992.
A set of articles utilizing contemporary critical models of interpretation: narrative, reader–response, deconstruction, feminist, and social criticisms.

237 E. V. McKnight. "Literary Criticism." Pp. 473–81 in *Dictionary of Jesus and the Gospels.* Edited by J. B. Green, S. McKnight, and I. H. Marshall. Downers Grove, Ill.: InterVaristy, 1992.
An introduction that focuses especially on the hermeneutical approaches emerging from postmodernism.

238 J. B. Tyson. *Images of Judaism in Luke–Acts.* Columbia: University of South Carolina, 1992.
Reads Luke–Acts utilizing reader–response criticism, namely, the implied reader.

239 D. H. Juel. *A Master of Surprise: Mark Interpreted.* Minneapolis: Fortress, 1994.

See #438.

240 E. K. Broadhead. "What are the Gospels? Questioning Martin Kähler." *Pacifica* 7 (1994): 145–59.

Challenges the conclusions of Martin Kähler with respect to the primacy of the kerygma over the pre-Passion material. Shows the impact of Kähler on Jesus studies, including his impact on narrative studies.

241 S. McKnight. "The Hermeneutics of Confessing Jesus as Lord." *Ex Auditu* 14 (1998): 1–17.

Challenges contemporary non-, a-, and anti-historical readings of Jesus and the Gospels; argues that early Christian faith was directed at Jesus and events of divine revelation in history, not the Christian "stories" about Jesus.

242 K. Vanhoozer. *Is There a Meaning in This Text? The Bible, the Reader, and the Morality of Literary Knowledge.* Grand Rapids: Zondervan, 1998.

A hermeneutically refined analysis of poststructuralism and deconstructive theories about literature and texts; proposes a determinate meaning in the text that transcends the surface text.

243 I. W. Batdorf. "Exercising the Canonical Option in the Quest for Jesus." *Evangelical Journal* 12 (1994): 51–59.

Historical Jesus studies attempt to create a Jesus other than the canonical Jesus; Jesus' life is to be understood in light of his death and resurrection; it leads into doxology.

3.7 Social-Scientific Studies

The most exciting recent phase of Gospel studies is the utilization of the social sciences, including cultural anthropology, sociology of knowledge, and sociology. While such studies transcend the more old-fashioned historical approach of "social description" by appealing to contemporary social-scientific models that allow the interpreter to "fill in the gaps," these studies appeal to current Gospels specialists because they are proving fruitful in answering previously unanswerable questions and by suggesting new avenues for inquiry. Two scholars have been utilized more than others: Peter Berger (see H. C. Kee) and Mary Douglass (B. J. Malina; J. H. Neyrey).

Connecting to the discussion of social-scientific studies is the utilization of "ideologies" to interpret the Gospels; here we come back to the fundamental perception that much of modern study is by white, Western males who think objectivity is what others see as bias. Hence, there are liberation and feminist examinations today of Jesus and the Gospels that challenge ideological presuppositions.

244 D. L. Tiede. *The Charismatic Figure as Miracle Worker.* SBLDS 1. Missoula: University of Montana for the Society of Biblical Literature, 1972.

A ground-breaking use of social types to explain Jesus and his presentations by the Evangelists. Studies the "divine wise man" in Hellenistic sources, Moses in Hellenistic Judaism, and Jesus as a "divine man."

245 J. G. Gager. *Kingdom and Community. The Social World of Early Christianity.* Prentice-Hall Studies in Religion Series. Englewood Cliffs, N.J.: Prentice-Hall, 1975.

One of the earliest applications of the social sciences to gospel studies. Gager argues that delay of the parousia actually provoked Christian intensity rather than discouraged it, as he saw elsewhere in other modern religious contexts.

246 H. C. Kee. *Community of the New Age. Studies in Mark's Gospel.* Philadelphia: Westminster, 1977.

The first major use of a sociological model for understanding the "community" of a Synoptist. See #424.

247 G. Theissen. *Sociology of Early Palestinian Christianity.* Philadelphia: Fortress, 1978. British edition: *The First Followers of Jesus.* London: SCM, 1978. Translated by J. Bowden. Original title: *Soziologie der Jesusbewegung.* München: Chr. Kaiser Verlag, 1977.

Seeks to analyze the social makeup of the earliest followers of Jesus. Using structural functionalism, the author argues that wandering charismatics were supported by local sympathizers as the paradigm for determining the social framework in which Jesus and the Gospels took shape. See the full-scale examination of R. A. Horsley, *Sociology and the Jesus Movement* (New York: Crossroad, 1989).

248 H. C. Kee. *Christian Origins in Sociological Perspective: Methods and Resources.* Philadelphia: Westminster, 1980.

Using the models of the development of a sect as fashioned by M. Weber, Kee offers separate studies on a "life world," leadership, identity, transformation of structural myth, and how the New Testament functioned socially.

249 B. J. Malina. *The New Testament World: Insights from Cultural Anthropology.* Louisville: Westminster/John Knox, 1981. Revised edition: 1993.
America's foremost user of social scientific theories. In this, his first book, he examines the role of shame/honor, first-century personality, the limited good, family, and purity. Malina's studies incited a new phase in Gospel studies in the use of social-scientific models.

250 H. C. Kee. *Miracle in the Early Christian World: A Study in Sociohistorical Method.* New Haven: Yale University Press, 1983.
Study of how miracles functioned in the ancient world with chapters on the apocalyptic tradition (Mark), history and romance (Luke), and universal symbol (John).

251 H. C. Kee. *Medicine, Miracle, and Magic in New Testament Times.* SNTSMS 55. Cambridge: Cambridge University Press, 1986.
Studies attitudes toward healing in Judaism and how medicine, magic, and miracle are understood within a worldview of God's control of humans.

252 B. J. Malina. *Christian Origins and Cultural Anthropology. Practical Models for Biblical Interpretation.* Atlanta: John Knox, 1986.
Applying the insights of Mary Douglass, in addition to a score of other socioanthropological theories, Malina analyzes the social makeup of earliest followers of Jesus along the line of cultural scripts.

253 W. A. Meeks. *The Moral World of the First Christians.* Library of Early Christianity. Philadelphia: Westminster, 1986.
Attempts to anchor the morals of Jesus and the Synoptic Gospels into the moral traditions of the Greco-Roman and Jewish traditions.

254 J. Schaberg. *The Illegitimacy of Jesus: A Feminist Theological Interpretation of the Infancy Narratives.* San Francisco: Harper & Row, 1987.
Skeptical, feminist study, concluding that Jesus was really born as an illegitimate child. Unfortunately, the study

embraces too many far-fetched explanations of critical issues, even if its ideological conclusions strike some important notes in our social setting. But see the author's response to (mostly over-)reactions to her study: J. Schaberg, "A Feminist Experience of Historical-Jesus Scholarship." Pp. 146–60 in *Whose Historical Jesus?* Studies in Christianity and Judaism 7. Edited by W. E. Arnal and M. Desjardins. Waterloo: Wilfrid Laurier University Press, 1997.

255 B. J. Malina and J. H. Neyrey. *Calling Jesus Names. The Social Value of Labels in Matthew.* Foundations & Facets. Social Facets. Sonoma, Calif.: Polebridge, 1988.
　　　An impressive use of the sociological model of "labeling"; see #349.

256 H. C. Kee. *Knowing the Truth: A Sociological Approach to New Testament Interpretation.* Minneapolis: Fortress, 1989.
　　　A survey for students of the growing bibliography of the use of sociological models for understanding the New Testament.

257 B. Holmberg. *Sociology and the New Testament: An Appraisal.* Minneapolis: Fortress, 1990.
　　　A clear-headed introduction to and evaluation of sociological models being used in New Testament scholarship.

258 W. R. Herzog II. "Sociological Approaches to the Gospels." Pp. 760–66 in *Dictionary of Jesus and the Gospels.* Edited by J. B. Green, S. McKnight, and I. H. Marshall. Downers Grove, Ill.: InterVarsity, 1992.
　　　Helpful survey and evaluation of how sociological tools are being used in Gospel studies.

259 J. R. Levison. "Liberation Hermeneutics." Pp. 464–69 in *Dictionary of Jesus and the Gospels.* Edited by J. B. Green, S. McKnight, and I. H. Marshall. Downers Grove, Ill.: InterVarsity, 1992.
　　　Demonstrates that the Gospels express a theme of liberation that has been used productively in liberation hermeneutics. Provides principles (e.g., no exegesis is objective) and surveys recent studies.

260 B. J. Malina and R. L. Rohrbaugh. *Social-Science Commentary on the Synoptic Gospels.* Minneapolis: Fortress, 1992.
　　　A pioneering attempt to highlight dimensions of the Synoptic Gospels that may be clarified by sociological models. Each section contains textual notes and "reading scenarios."

261 J. H. Elliott. *What is Social-Scientific Criticism?* Philadelphia: Fortress, 1993.

A useful student guide to how social-scientific criticism is being done in New Testament studies.

262 J. K. Chance. "The Anthropology of Honor and Shame: Culture, Values, and Practice." *Semeia* 68 (1994): 139–51.

A challenge to Synoptic scholars using the models of "honor and shame"; argues that anthropologists do not agree on definitions about the concepts in the ancient Mediterranean world and that different ancient cultures should not be homogenized.

263 H. C. Kee. *Who are the People of God? Early Christian Models of Community.* New Haven/London: Yale University Press, 1995.

Explications of early Christian adaptations of Jewish models of community to identify themselves as the people of God. Mark utilizes "wisdom," Matthew "law-abiding," and Luke "cultural and ethnic inclusion."

264 J. Dewey. "From Storytelling to Written Text: The Loss of Early Christian Women's Voices." *Biblical Theology Bulletin* 26 (1996): 71–78.

The freezing of the oral tradition by canonical decisions, all made by men, eclipsed the role women played in storytelling; the Gospels show the reduction of women's voices.

265 B. J. Malina. *The Social World of Jesus and the Gospels.* London: Routledge, 1996.

A collection of mostly previously published essays; note especially the study of Jesus and Mary (pp. 97–120), Jesus (not) as a charismatic leader (pp. 123–42), and patron–client relations as the structural foundation of Synoptic theology (pp. 143–75).

3.8 Genre Criticism

Genre investigation this century began with the assumption the Gospels were "ancient biographies." However, with the rise of form criticism and redaction criticism came the conviction that the Gospels were in fact theological treatises and belonged to the realm of "kerygma" and not historiography. "Gospel" then emerges from the kerygma and is *sui generis.* A more careful examination of both Gospel "genre" and ancient biographies *(bioi)*, however, has led the conversation full circle: today scholars see the Gospels as "biographies" in the Greco-Roman model although most are keen to point to how different the Gospels are when compared to the biographies of the ancient world.

266 C. W. Votaw. "The Gospels and Contemporary Biographies." *American Journal of Theology* 19 (1915): 45–73, 217–49. Reprinted in *The Gospels and Contemporary Biographies in the Graeco-Roman World.* Facet Book. Biblical Series 27. Philadelphia: Fortress, 1970.
An early proposal that sought the genre of the Gospels in Greco-Roman biographies, which were used for hortatory purposes.

267 H. C. Kee. "Aretalogy and Gospel." *JBL* 92 (1972): 402–22.
Critiques the thesis held by some (including Morton Smith, "Prolegomena to a Discussion of Aretalogies, Divine Men, the Gospels, and Jesus," *JBL* 90 [1971]: 179–99) that the Gospels are aretalogies—collections of miracle stories that divinize a hero.

268 G. N. Stanton. *Jesus of Nazareth in New Testament Preaching.* SNTSMS 27. New York: Cambridge University Press, 1974.
Contends that the historical Jesus was always part of the preaching of the earliest churches; the Gospels then contain a genuinely historical interest.

269 R. H. Gundry. "Recent Investigations into the Literary Genre 'Gospel.'" Pp. 97–114 in *New Dimensions in New Testament Study.* Edited by R. N. Longenecker and M. C. Tenney. Grand Rapids: Zondervan, 1974.
Lucid survey of the history of the genre question of the Gospels. One should not speak of a genre "gospel" but of the presence of "gospels," early Christian attempts to be both historical and theological about Jesus.

270 G. G. Bilezikian. *The Liberated Gospel: A Comparison of the Gospel of Mark and Greek Tragedy.* Grand Rapids: Baker, 1977.
An early (and usually neglected) attempt to relate the Gospel of Mark to the Greek genre of tragedy, other than ancient biographies. Argues that Mark is best explained as Greek tragedy. "Tragedy was the consecrated medium for contemplating the mysterious outworkings of fate and affirming the ultimate triumph of humane and righteous causes over . . . unjust forces" (p. 144).

271 C. H. Talbert. *What is a Gospel? The Genre of the Canonical Gospels.* Philadelphia: Fortress, 1977.

A significant and influential resurrection of the "biography" hypothesis. Responds to the Bultmann argument against "biography": the presence of myth. Finds five functions of ancient biographies and relates the Gospels to one of those.

272 P. L. Shuler. *A Genre for the Gospels: The Biographical Character of Matthew.* Philadelphia: Fortress, 1982.

Surveys the history of discussion; the Gospels are "laudatory biographies" (encomia). This proposal has been widely accepted. See #287.

273 R. Guelich. "The Gospel Genre." Pp. 173–208 in *The Gospel and the Gospels.* Edited by P. Stuhlmacher. Grand Rapids: Eerdmans, 1991. Original title: *Das Evangelium und die Evangelien. Vorträge vom Tübingen Symposium 1982.* WUNT 28. Tübingen: J. C. B. Mohr, 1983.

An exhaustive survey of the history of discussion. Revives the German view that the Gospels are their own genre: (1) formally, an account of the public life of Jesus; (2) formally, the structure derives from early Christian preaching about God's salvation in Jesus Christ; (3) materially, they make a statement about God and Jesus Christ. The material content led to their anonymity.

274 G. N. Stanton. "Matthew as a Creative Interpreter of the Sayings of Jesus." Pp. 257–72 in *The Gospel and the Gospels.* Edited by P. Stuhlmacher. Grand Rapids: Eerdmans, 1991. Original title: *Das Evangelium und die Evangelien. Vorträge vom Tübingen Symposium 1982.* WUNT 28. Tübingen: J. C. B. Mohr, 1983.

Examines the expansions by Matthew of his sources. Matthew is creative but he is not innovative. Both Mark and Matthew can be labeled "Gospel."

275 R. T. France and D. Wenham (eds.). *Studies in Midrash and Historiography.* Gospel Perspectives 3. Sheffield: JSOT, 1983.

The rising tide of using "midrash" to explain Gospel traditions meets a breakwater; scholars include B. D. Chilton, R. Bauckham, F. F. Bruce, R. T. France, L. L. Morris, D. J. Moo, P. B. Payne, and C. L. Blomberg.

276 D. E. Aune. *The New Testament in Its Literary Environment.* Library of Early Christianity. Philadelphia: Westminster, 1988.

Recognizes the nuances of the different Gospels in genre classification; sees them as subtypes of biographies; Luke–Acts belongs with "general history."

277   H. Koester. *Ancient Christian Gospels: Their History and Development.* London: SCM/Philadelphia: Trinity Press International, 1990.

> See #45.

278   E. E. Lemcio. *The Past of Jesus in the Gospels.* SNTSMS 68. Cambridge: Cambridge University Press, 1991.

> The Evangelists consciously distinguished their own setting (and theological vocabulary) from that of Jesus; this is visible in an idiom that reflects a "past" rather than a present. Appendix on the unifying kerygma of New Testament theology.

279   R. A. Burridge *What are the Gospels? A Comparison with Graeco-Roman Biography.* SNTSMS 70. Cambridge: Cambridge University Press, 1992.

> Careful linguistic comparison of the Gospels with Greco-Roman biographies. Examines opening features, subject, external features, and internal features. Concludes that "there is a high correlation between the generic features of Graeco-Roman biographies *(bioi)* and those of the synoptic gospels" (p. 218).

280   L. W. Hurtado. "Gospel (Genre)." Pp. 276–82 in *Dictionary of Jesus and the Gospels.* Edited by J. B. Green, S. McKnight, and I. H. Marshall. Downers Grove, Ill.: InterVarsity, 1992.

> Balanced survey of the discussion and the main issues to be analyzed; presents the genre in both formal and functional terms.

281   G. Strecker. *History of New Testament Literature.* Translated by C. Katter, with H. Mollenhauer. Harrisburg, Pa.: Trinity Press International, 1997. Original title: *Literaturgeschichte des Neuen Testaments.* Göttingen: Vandenhoeck & Ruprecht, 1992.

> Attempts to transcend the limitations of a strictly canonical approach. Examines "gospel" in terms of tradition-history and source criticism as a special modification of ancient biographies.

282   A. F. J. Klijn. *Jewish-Christian Gospel Tradition.* Supplements to Vigiliae Christianae 17. Leiden: E. J. Brill, 1992.

> Complete presentation of the evidence for "Jewish-Christian" gospels in the early churches and a discussion of their contents. Provides text and commentary on the evidence.

283   G. E. Sterling. *Historiography and Self-Definition: Josephos, Luke–Acts and Apologetic Historiography.* NovTestSuppl 64. Leiden: E. J. Brill, 1992.

Luke fits into the attempts of others in the Mediterranean who rewrote the history of a people in a Hellenized form; the "lack of antiquity" is overcome by appeal to continuity with ancient Israel.

284 E. S. B. Shim. "A Suggestion about the Genre or Text-Type of Mark." *Scriptura* 50 (1994): 69–89.

Mark needs to be seen as a "new genre" that combines literary and rhetorical strategies; one of the few studies of genre that incorporates the insights of aesthetics studies.

285 I. H. Jones. *The Matthean Parables. A Literary and Historical Commentary.* NovTestSuppl 80. Leiden: E. J. Brill, 1995.

Extensive study of Matthew's parables along literary lines in order to shed light on the question of Matthew's "genre." Finds a new genre on the basis of the spirituality Matthew's parables generate.

286 R. H. Gundry. "ΕΥΑΓΓΕΛΙΟΝ: How Soon a Book?" *JBL* 115 (1996): 321–25.

Brief description of evidence used to contend that "gospel" was a term for a book; argues that there is no evidence before Marcion.

4

The Gospel of Matthew

Matthew's Gospel has moved in the twentieth century from being understood as a Jewish depiction of the "life of Jesus" to the product of a sophisticated theologian engaged in both literary art and polemical debate with contemporary Judaism. Primary debates today involve the setting of Matthew (in particular, whether Matthew's "community" remains within Judaism as a sect or outside Judaism as a new religious movement) as well as discussion of its Christology, ecclesiology, ethic, and structure. Several studies of late have been devoted to its literary art; others have moved into other "aesthetic models" of critical study.

4.0 Introductory Issues (Author, Date, Purpose, Audience)

No consensus exists on the author: while traditional scholars contend the apostle is responsible for the First Gospel, critical scholars find the "use" of Mark in Matthew's version of his own conversion (cf. Matt. 9:9–13) quite unlikely. Most today date the Gospel after the destruction of Jerusalem, usually within about a decade. The provenance of Matthew has been hotly disputed, with the most recent studies arguing that Matthew's community was situated in Syrian Antioch.

287 P. L. Shuler. *A Genre for the Gospels: The Biographical Character of Matthew.* Philadelphia: Fortress, 1982.

Surveys the history of discussion; the Gospels are "laudatory biographies" (encomia). This proposal has been widely accepted.

288 G. Stanton (ed.). *The Interpretation of Matthew.* Issues in Religion and Theology 3. Philadelphia: Fortress/London: SPCK, 1983. Second edition: Edinburgh: T. & T. Clark, 1995.

An important collection of influential studies that shape the contemporary discussion of Matthew. Second edition extends introduction and adds an article on literary criticism.

289 G. N. Stanton. "The Origin and Purpose of Matthew's Gospel: Matthean Scholarship from 1945 to 1980." Pp. 1889–1951 in *Aufstieg und Niedergang der römischen Welt.* 2.25.3. Edited by H. Temporini and W. Haase. Berlin: W. de Gruyter, 1983.

The most comprehensive study of the *Sitz im Leben* of Matthew; surveys critical methodology; relationship to other Christian groups and to Judaism; theology; origins. Contends Matthew is outside Judaism but defines itself over against Judaism.

290 G. Howard. *The Gospel of Matthew according to a Primitive Hebrew Text.* Macon, Ga.: Mercer University Press, 1987. Second edition: *Hebrew Gospel of Matthew,* 1995.

Examines a fourteenth-century Jewish polemical treatise *(Even Bohan)* and argues that the Hebrew text of Matthew in it reveals an evolutionary development. The Hebrew is what one expects of a first-century text; concludes that both the Greek Matthew and this Hebrew Matthew (the old substratum) are each original compositions (not related to one another), the Hebrew possibly even earlier than our Greek Matthew. The second edition corrects the text and slightly revises the work in light of the author's own studies.

291 R. T. France. *Matthew: Evangelist and Teacher.* Grand Rapids: Zondervan, 1989. Reprinted Downers Grove, Ill.: InterVarsity, 1998.

Surveys the main themes of Matthew's theology and the recent discussions in Matthean interpretation. Especially helpful on Christology.

292 D. L. Balch (ed.). *Social History of the Matthean Community: Cross-Disciplinary Approaches.* Minneapolis: Fortress, 1991.

Papers from a conference on the setting of Matthew held at Southern Methodist University in 1989. A notable feature of the conference is the emerging consensus that Christian and

Jewish scholars must work together. Four issues are discussed: (1) Jewish and Hellenistic aspects; (2) women in an agrarian society; (3) Matthew and Ignatius of Antioch; (4) the social situation and location.

293   S. McKnight. "Matthew, Gospel of." Pp. 526–41 in *Dictionary of Jesus and the Gospels*. Edited by J. B. Green, S. McKnight, and I. H. Marshall. Downers Grove, Ill.: InterVarsity, 1992.

Brief study on introductory issues and theology of Matthew. Offers a methodology and proposal for structural considerations; suggests that Matthew's Christology is best understood functionally, rather than titularly; examines the "periods" of Matthew's salvation history.

294   A. J. Saldarini. *Matthew's Christian-Jewish Community*. Chicago/London: University of Chicago Press, 1994.

A Jewish-Christian movement that has not yet separated from Judaism; uses sociological methods. See #360.

295   S. McKnight. "Matthean Community." Pp. 724–29 in *Dictionary of the Later New Testament and Its Developments*. Edited by R. P. Martin and P. H. Davids. Downers Grove, Ill.: InterVarsity, 1997.

Surveys contemporary discussion of Matthew's *Sitz im Leben* and proposes a methodology for determining Matthew's *Sitz im Leben*; argues that Matthew's community has been ostracized from the synagogue, was debating the nature of the true Israel with the Pharisees, but was still within Judaism.

296   S. P. Kealy. *Matthew's Gospel and the History of Biblical Interpretation*. Mellen Biblical Press Series 55. 2 volumes. Lewiston/Queenston: Edwin Mellen, 1997.

Exhaustive survey of the history of interpretation; divides the history by periods and by hermeneutical approaches.

297   R. F. Shedinger. "The Textual Relationship between P^{45} and Shem-Tob's Hebrew Matthew." *NTS* 43 (1997): 58–71.

Confirms the theory of Howard (#290) by arguing a connection between the third century manuscript and the Hebrew substratum of Shem-Tob.

298   D. C. Sim. *The Gospel of Matthew and Christian Judaism*. Edinburgh: T. & T. Clark, 1998.

Argues that Matthew's community was still within Judaism, that the Gospel emerges from what is known about Antioch, and that the community is anti-Pauline.

4.1 Commentaries

Matthew has been served well by commentators; a veritable history of Synoptics studies can be traced in the methodologies of the commentators. Included here are a few commentaries on the Sermon on the Mount as well as some homiletical treatments of Matthew.

299 W. C. Allen. *A Critical and Exegetical Commentary on the Gospel according to S. Matthew.* Edinburgh: T. & T. Clark, 1907. Third edition: 1912.

A definitive commentary in its time, this work is now most useful for delineating Matthew's sources. Part of Sanday's famous Seminar (see #115).

300 A. H. McNeile. *The Gospel according to Matthew: The Greek Text with Introduction, Notes, and Indices.* London: Macmillan, 1915. Reprinted Grand Rapids: Baker, 1980. Thornapple Commentaries.

Classic study that focuses on grammar, syntax, and history.

301 W. Grundmann. *Das Evangelium nach Matthäus.* Theologischer Handkommentar zum Neuen Testament. Berlin: Evangelische Verlagsanstalt, 1968. Fifth edition: 1981.

Comprehensive, penetrating commentary that contributes considerably to the Old Testament background to the First Gospel. Grundmann was anti-Semitic. See S. Heschel, "Nazifying Christian Theology: Walter Grundmann and the Institute for the Study and Eradication of Jewish Influence on German Church Life." *Church History* 63 (1994): 587–605.

302 D. Hill. *The Gospel of Matthew.* New Century Bible. London: Marshall, Morgan & Scott/Grand Rapids: Eerdmans, 1972.

Very much along the lines of P. Bonnard's French commentary; brings Matthew studies up to date on recent discussions about Jesus and Matthew's theology.

303 E. Schweizer. *The Good News according to Matthew.* Translated by D. E. Green. Atlanta: John Knox, 1975. Original title: *Das Evangelium nach Matthäus.* NTD 2. Göttingen: Vandenhoeck & Ruprecht, 1973.

Lucid, insightful study on the structure, composition, and theology of the First Gospel.

304 J. P. Meier. *Matthew.* New Testament Message 3. Wilmington, Del.: Michael Glazier, 1980.

Lucid survey by a leading Roman Catholic Matthean scholar. Especially helpful on structural flow and theological context.

305 P. Bonnard. *L'Évangile selon Saint Matthieu.* Commentaire du Nouveau Testament Deuxième Série 1. Genève: Labor et Fides, 1982.
Brilliant study of Matthew's historical context and theological ideas; aware of European scholarship; grammatical.

306 R. A. Guelich. *The Sermon on the Mount: A Foundation for Understanding.* Waco: Word Books, 1982.
Exhaustive, tradition-critical. The most complete commentary available to English readers. Offers full interaction with critical scholarship.

307 R. H. Gundry. *Matthew: A Commentary on His Literary and Theological Art.* Grand Rapids: Eerdmans, 1982. Second edition: 1994.
Exhaustive study of Matthew's redactional habits and tendencies. Overly reliant upon word statistics; second edition interacts some with contemporary scholarship. Indispensable for the serious student. Generated massive debate within evangelicalism on the place of midrash and redaction.

308 L. Sabourin, S. J. *The Gospel according to St Matthew.* 2 volumes. Bombay, India: St. Paul, 1982.
Little-known, but refreshingly complete and independent. Especially helpful for understanding Matthew's theology. By a veteran Roman Catholic scholar who has written extensively in New Testament studies.

309 D. A. Carson. "Matthew." *Expositor's Bible Commentary.* Volume 8. Grand Rapids: Zondervan, 1984.
Comprehensive, exegetical, and homiletical. Critical of most recent scholarship on the First Gospel. Useful especially for evangelical preachers.

310 R. T. France. *The Gospel according to Matthew: An Introduction and Commentary.* Tyndale New Testament Commentary 1. Leicester: InterVarsity/Grand Rapids: Eerdmans, 1985.
Fresh, insightful, if brief. A first-class Matthean scholar writes with the evangelical Bible student in mind.

311 U. Luz. *Matthew 1–7: A Commentary.* Translated by W. C. Linss. Minneapolis: Augsburg Fortress, 1989. Original title: *Das Evangelium nach Matthäus,* 1. Teilband, *Mt 1–7.* Evangelisch-Katholischer Kommentar zum Neuen Testament. Zurich: Benziger Verlag, 1985.

Exhaustive, exegetical, and critical. Adds sections at times on how a particular text has been used in various ways in the history of the Church. See #359 below. Especially helpful for discerning Matthew's redactional theology. Helpful bibliographies; reflects contemporary German, critical scholarship.

312 C. Bauman. *The Sermon on the Mount: The Modern Quest for Its Meaning.* Macon, Ga.: Mercer University Press, 1985.
Examines the Sermon's interpretation by nineteen (mostly German) scholars; treats L. Tolstoy, A. Schweitzer, R. Kittel, R. Bultmann, H. Windisch, D. Bonhoeffer, and J. Jeremias. A good place to begin study of the Sermon's history of interpretation.

313 J. Gnilka. *Das Matthäusevangelium.* Herders Theologischer Kommentar zum Neuen Testament. 2 volumes. Freiburg: Herder, 1986, 1988.
Exhaustive, exegetical, and critical. Especially concerned with the underlying traditions of Matthew and how Matthew has shaped them. Provides complete bibliographies and emphasizes German scholarship.

314 D. Patte. *The Gospel according to Matthew: A Structural Commentary on Matthew's Faith.* Philadelphia: Fortress, 1987.
Examines Matthew from a structuralist angle; contribution is minimal but at times refreshing and insightful.

315 W. D. Davies and D. C. Allison Jr. *A Critical and Exegetical Commentary on The Gospel according to Saint Matthew.* International Critical Commentary. 3 volumes. Edinburgh: T. & T. Clark, 1988, 1991, 1997.
Magisterial, exhaustive, exegetical, historical, critical. Unparalleled in its contribution for the serious student. Emphasizes the historical-theological context out of which and to which Matthew spoke.

316 D. A. Hagner. *Matthew 1–13. Matthew 14–28.* Word Biblical Commentary 33A, 33B. Dallas: Word Books, 1993, 1997.
Comprehensive, scholarly, exegetical, and historically sensitive. Exhaustive bibliographies. Useful for students and scholars alike. Especially suitable for those inquiring into Matthew's theological orientation.

317 J. H. Charlesworth, M. Harding, and M. Kiley (eds.). *The Lord's Prayer and Other Prayer Texts from the Greco-Roman Era.* Valley Forge, Pa.: Trinity Press International, 1994.

Technical studies on prayer in the ancient world (on *Abba*, the Lord's Prayer, Simeon's prayer, prayers in Josephus, 1 Maccabees, and 1 Clement 59:3–61:3) are followed by an exhaustive bibliography on the Lord's Prayer and ancient prayers by M. Kiley.

318 H. D. Betz. *The Sermon on the Mount: A Commentary on the Sermon on the Mount, including the Sermon on the Plain (Matthew 5:3–7:27 and Luke 6:20–49).* Hermeneia. Minneapolis: Fortress, 1995.

An exhaustive, old-fashioned form-critical, speculative source-critical and rhetorical analysis. Complete control of technical bibliography and sources. The variant of Q Matthew inherited (QMatt) already had the Sermon on the Mount while Luke's Q (QLuke) had the Sermon on the Plain. Matthew's presentation betrays a community still within Judaism while Luke's sermon reveals a more Hellenized theology. Command of the Greco-Roman sources fills in a gap.

319 J. A. Overman. *Church and Community in Crisis: The Gospel according to Matthew.* New Testament in Context. Valley Forge, Pa.: Trinity Press International, 1996.

Readable, socially informed commentary; attempts to explain Matthew as a community in crisis with Judaism. The community offered a solution to the problems of Galilean society.

4.2 Special Studies

The rise of redaction criticism shifted the interests of scholars away from the Gospel of Mark and toward the "redactional contributions" of the individual Evangelists. Not only had the Gospel of Matthew enjoyed a favorite position among the earliest churches but in modern studies it established itself as a test case for every new methodological orientation. Alongside traditional, historical studies of Matthew, discoveries in the deserts of Judea led to an intense and growing discussion of Matthew's use of the Old Testament (see Stendahl, #320) while the insightful suggestions of G. Bornkamm (#325) in a few essays spawned a massive industry of redaction-critical studies of Matthew's theology and setting. The emergence of composition and literary/narrative criticism, which moved beyond the redactional distinctives to a larger presentation of Matthew's theology and text, spearheaded largely by J. D. Kingsbury (#368) and his students, dominated Matthean scholarship in the United States for over a decade. Scholarship today is fragmented in methodological orientation but there is undoubtedly a turn toward a more historical orientation to Matthew's Gospel, seen especially in the edited collection of Balch (#292) and the massive commentary of D. C. Allison Jr. (#315). It has not always been easy to distinguish between redaction-critical and historical studies.

4.2.1 Use of the Old Testament

320 K. Stendahl. *The School of St. Matthew and Its Use of the Old Testament.* Acta Seminarii Neotestamentici Upsaliensis 20. Lund: C. W. K. Gleerup, 1954. Second edition: 1967. Reprinted Mifflintown, Pa.: Sigler Press, 1991.

Matthew was intended to be a handbook for liturgical and catechetical purposes; derives from a school where an ingenious method *(pesher)* of interpreting the Old Testament evolved.

321 R. H. Gundry. *The Use of the Old Testament in St. Matthew's Gospel, with Special Reference to the Messianic Hope.* NovTestSuppl 18. Leiden: E. J. Brill, 1975.

Matthew essentially uses the LXX when he quotes the Old Testament formally; a mixed tradition is found elsewhere in Matthew. Matthew was a targumist and a note-taker during the life of Jesus; such notes are the foundation of the Gospel traditions. Challenges the form-critical orientation.

322 O. L. Cope. *Matthew: A Scribe Trained for the Kingdom of Heaven.* Catholic Biblical Quarterly Monograph Series 5. Washington, D.C.: The Catholic Biblical Association of America, 1976.

Matthew was a Jewish Christian conversant with both Old Testament and Jewish hermeneutics; Matthew is thus a "scribe trained for the Kingdom"; examines key texts.

323 G. M. S. Prabhu. *The Formula Quotations in the Infancy Narrative of Matthew. An Inquiry into the Tradition History of Mt 1–2.* Analecta Biblica 63. Rome: Biblical Institute Press, 1976.

The formula quotations of Matthew 1–2 are a special creation of Matthew; they are free, targumic renderings of an original Hebrew text shaped to the context of Matthew in light of his Christology. The surrounding narratives emerge from various traditions and sources, but are not Matthean creations.

4.2.2 Redaction-Critical and Theological Studies

324 W. Trilling. *Das wahre Israel: Studien zur Theologie des Matthäus-Evangeliums.* Studien zum Alten und Neuen Testament 10. München: Kösel-Verlag, 1959. Third edition: 1964.

Early, influential study of the particular contribution Matthew makes to the Jesus traditions; examines Matthew 28:18–10; 21:33–45 (21:43 is redactional); 27:15–26 (emphasizes Jewish guilt); the judgment on Israel (polemic over the identity of Israel); 10:5–6; 15:24 (mission restricted to Israel to emphasize their guilt); 18:1–35; theology of the church (universal presence of the kingdom) and the Law (maintained but neutralized). The will of God is found in perfection and love. Church is the "true" Israel and the book stems from a Jewish milieu.

325 G. Bornkamm, G. Barth, and H. J. Held. *Tradition and Interpretation in Matthew.* The New Testament Library. Translated by P. Scott. Philadelphia: Westminster/London: SCM, 1963. Original title: *Überlieferung und Auslegung im Matthäusevangelium.* Wissenschaftliche Monographien zum Alten und Neuen Testaments 1. Neukirchen: Neukirchener Verlag, 1960.

Reprints two discipline-shaping essays of G. Bornkamm on the expectation of the end and the church and on the stilling of the storm; contains the dissertations of two of his students (Barth, Held). Barth's study of the Law emphasizes the place of love and discipleship as grids through which the Law must be interpreted. Held's presentation of miracles, still fundamental, reveals that Matthew's redactional interest is in Christology and faith.

326 G. Strecker. *Der Weg der Gerechtigkeit. Untersuchung zur Theologie des Matthäus.* Göttingen: Vandenhoeck & Ruprecht, 1962. Third edition: 1971.

After a detailed analysis of the citation formulas, examines Christology and ecclesiology to show that Matthew redactionally locates Jesus in a special time in salvation-history (historicization): after the resurrection it is the time of the church. Concern for salvation-history emerges from the work of O. Cullmann and H. Conzelmann (#480).

327 R. Walker. *Die Heilsgeschichte im ersten Evangelium.* Forschungen zur Religion und Literatur des Alten und Neuen Testaments 91. Göttingen: Vandenhoeck & Ruprecht, 1967.

Salvation-history study. Matthew's age is the "age of the Gentile mission" with three periods of salvation-history: (1) prehistory of the Messiah, (2) history of the call of Israel, (3) the mission to the Gentiles.

328 M. J. Suggs. *Wisdom, Christology, and Law in Matthew's Gospel.* Cambridge, Mass.: Harvard University Press, 1970.

Attempts to show that Wisdom speculation has a decisive role to play in Matthew's Christology; examines especially Matthew 11:2–19; 11:28–30; 23:37–39. Integrates Wisdom and Law; Jesus is here *identified* with Wisdom.

329 A. Sand. *Das Gesetz und die Propheten. Untersuchungen zur Theologie des Evangeliums nach Matthäus.* Biblische Untersuchungen 11. Edited by Otto Kuss. Regensburg: F. Pustet, 1974.

Examines the themes of the Law and the prophetic dimension of Matthew's theology. The revelation of God was expressed to Israel in the Torah but it is best perceived from its "weightier demands"; emphasis on love, compassion, and the needs of others derives from Israel's prophets. Too complex and general to focus on only one group or *Sitz im Leben.*

330 J. P. Meier. *Law and History in Matthew's Gospel.* Analecta Biblica 71. Rome: Biblical Institute Press, 1976.

Focuses on Matthew 5:17–48, with special attention on 5:17–20. Death and resurrection complex is understood as the crucial turning point in salvation-history.

331 D. E. Garland. *The Intention of Matthew 23.* NovTestSuppl 52. Leiden: E. J. Brill, 1979.

Intense examination of Matthew 23. After proposing a structure, he argues that chapter 23 was directed at disciple leaders in the church of Matthew; "woes" are tantamount to a "curse"; "hypocrisy" is a complex accusation against the leaders for subverting God's will by false interpretation. Model dissertation.

332 B. M. Nolan. *The Royal Son of God: The Christology of Matthew 1–2 in the Setting of the Gospel.* Orbis Biblicus et Orientalis 23. Göttingen: Vandenhoeck & Ruprecht, 1979.

Argues against the "Son of God" emphasis; proposes a "royal, davidic" Christology as the surest synthesis of Matthew's Christology.

333 D. P. Senior. *The Passion Narrative according to Matthew: A Redactional Study.* BETL 39. Leuven: Leuven University Press, 1982.

An early redaction-critical commentary on Matthew 26–28.

334 S. H. Brooks. *Matthew's Community: The Evidence of His Special Sayings Material.* JSNTSS 16. Sheffield: JSOT, 1987.

Intense tradition-critical study of the "M" traditions; not enough data to posit a written source but one can see a development of the "M" traditions. Matthew perceives Christian history through its relationship to synagogal authorities.

335 W. L. Kynes. *A Christology of Solidarity: Jesus as the Representative of His People in Matthew.* Lanham, Md.: University Press of America, 1991.

Jesus stands between Israel and the church, functioning as the representative of both. He is the ideal Son of God that Israel was meant to be as well as the one who stands both *over* and *with* the church.

336 B. Charette. *The Theme of Recompense in Matthew's Gospel.* JSNTSS 79. Sheffield: JSOT, 1992.

Elucidates the (Sinaitic) covenant background for Matthew's emphasis on reward and punishment; special attention is given to the theme of the land as appropriated spiritually by the church.

337 J. Neusner. *A Rabbi Talks with Jesus: An Intermillennial Interfaith Exchange.* London: Doubleday, 1993.

The author, a famous Jewish scholar, tells his readers why he would not have joined the Jesus movement had he lived in the first century. When Jesus differs with Moses, Neusner sides with Moses.

338 M. Knowles. *Jeremiah in Matthew's Gospel: The Rejected Prophet Motif in Matthaean Redaction.* JSNTSS 68. Sheffield: JSOT, 1993.

Examines Matthew 2:17–18 (Jer. 31:15); 16:13–20; and 27:9–10 (Jer. 32:6–15) and how these Jeremiah passages impact the Christology of Matthew. Like Jeremiah, Jesus was a rejected prophet and Matthew's community drew upon this theme in light of the destruction of Jerusalem.

339 G. Häfner. *Der verheissene Vorläufer. Redaktionsgeschichtliche Untersuchung zur Darstellung Johannes der Täufer im Matthäus-Evangelium.* Stuttgarter Biblische Beiträge 27. Stuttgart: Katholisches Bibelwerk, 1994.

Thorough analysis of the John the Baptist pericopes and themes in Matthew; Matthew emphasizes the correlation of John and Jesus and draws out the significance of John's connections with Elijah.

340 K. G. C. Newport. *The Sources and* Sitz im Leben *of Matthew 23.* JSNTSS 117. Sheffield: Sheffield Academic, 1995.

Redaction- and source-critical examination of Matthew 23; determines that most derives from a single early polemic treatise (vv. 2–31); shows that it emerges from within Judaism and that all of it is compatible with Judaism prior to the First Jewish Revolt.

341 C. M. Deutsch. *Lady Wisdom, Jesus, and the Sages: Metaphor and Social Context in Matthew's Gospel.* Valley Forge, Pa.: Trinity Press International, 1996.

Examines the theme in biblical and Jewish sources. Elucidates the manner in which Matthew makes use of the Wisdom motif; connects Wisdom to Jesus' teaching; Wisdom is identified with Jesus to establish the superiority of Matthew's teaching.

4.2.3 Historical and Social-Scientific Studies

342 W. D. Davies. *The Setting of the Sermon on the Mount.* Cambridge: Cambridge University Press, 1964. Reprinted in Brown Judaic Studies 186. Atlanta, Ga.: Scholars, 1989.

Argues that Matthew's Sermon on the Mount originated in the dialogue and conflict of Matthew with Judaism just after A.D. 70. A book of uncommon penetration and methodological precision. Davies wrote when Christian use of Jewish sources was in its infancy. Matthew is seen as presenting Jesus as the giver of new laws and as the New Moses (see also #356). The Sermon is a Christian response to the events in Judaism centering in Jamnia (Yavneh).

343 D. R. A. Hare. *The Theme of Jewish Persecution of Christians in the Gospel according to St. Matthew.* SNTSMS 6. Cambridge: Cambridge University Press, 1967.

Shaped Matthean studies by exploring social dimensions rather than just theological ones in the debate with Judaism. Persecution of the Christians was not institutional but local and sporadic; only Matthew's "missionaries" were persecuted. Church replaces Israel in Matthean theology.

344 B. Przybylski. *Righteousness in Matthew and His World of Thought.* SNTSMS 41. Cambridge: Cambridge University Press, 1980.

The determinate study of "righteousness" in Matthew; the term is a "provisional" concept and used as a point of contact between Judaism (largely derived from Qumran and the Tannaim) and Matthean theology. Term denotes the demand of God upon humans for proper religious behavior; the better "Christian" expression is "doing the will of God."

345 R. Mohrlang. *Matthew and Paul: A Comparison of Ethical Perspectives.* SNTSMS 48. Cambridge: Cambridge University Press, 1984.

Fair-minded attempt to set Matthew's theology over against Paul's in their own terms; given the "language game" of each, the substance remains compatible. Each derives theology from Christology but each also has distinctive emphases. Comparison of early "varieties" of Christian faith; sees diversity within a unity.

346 P. Sigal. *The Halakah of Jesus of Nazareth according to the Gospel of Matthew.* Lanham, Md.: University Press of America, 1986.

Matthew needs to be set into the historical development of halakah from the Old Testament to the Mishnah by examining his "halakah" regarding divorce and Sabbath; Jesus is a proto-rabbi for Matthew. The Pharisees of Matthew are a small separatistic group best compared to Qumranites and those behind *Jubilees.*

347 P. S. Cameron. *Violence and the Kingdom: The Interpretation of Matthew 11:12.* Arbeiten zum Neuen Testament und Judentum 5. Frankfurt am Main: Peter Lang, 1984. Second edition: 1988.

A comprehensive analysis of the history of interpretation of this vexed logion which originally described John the Baptist's treatment at the hands of Herod Antipas.

348 A.-J. Levine. *The Social and Ethnic Dimensions of Matthean Salvation History: "Go Nowhere among the Gentiles . . ." (Matt. 10:5b).* Studies in the Bible and Early Christianity 14. Lewiston/Queenston: Edwin Mellen, 1988.

Utilizes redaction, sociological, and feminist criticism to establish a historically sensitive context for Matthew's theology; issue is not Jew versus Gentile but powerful versus powerless. Ethnic categories have been rendered inoperative by Matthew. Salvation-history has a temporal (post–Great Commission universalism) and social (ethnicity denied) axis.

349 B. J. Malina and J. H. Neyrey. *Calling Jesus Names: The Social Value of Labels in Matthew.* Foundations & Facets. Social Facets. Sonoma, Calif.: Polebridge, 1988.

The first social-scientific study of Matthew; exceptionally insightful. Studies the social function of "labeling" a "prominent" (Jesus); Jesus is labeled a "deviant" by his opponents but a "prominent" by his followers. Focuses on Matthew 12 and 26–27.

350 M. J. Wilkins. *The Concept of Disciple in Matthew's Gospel: As Reflected in the Use of the Term* Μαθητης. NovTestSuppl 59. Leiden: E. J. Brill, 1988.

Detailed "word-study" examination of "disciple" in (1) the classical and Hellenistic background, (2) the Old Testament, and (3) intertestamental texts. Term was a favorite because it expressed the relationship of an "adherent to a great teacher" more than a "learner"; examines the term in light of a literary-critical approach and how Peter fits into that paradigm.

351 D. E. Orton. *The Understanding Scribe: Matthew and the Apocalyptic Ideal.* JSNTSS 25. Sheffield: JSOT, 1989.

Examines the "scribal ideal" in the ancient world of Judaism (Old Testament, Second Temple, Ben Sira, apocalyptic literature, and Qumran). Matthew's presentation of "scribe" fits especially into the nonrabbinic and non-Pharisaic sources; Pharisaic scribes are criticized because they fail to attain Matthew's perception of the "ideal scribe." Use of "scribe" for disciples intentionally conforms to the apocalyptic ideal.

352 J. A. Overman. *Matthew's Gospel and Formative Judaism. The Social World of the Matthean Community.* Minneapolis: Fortress, 1990.

Uses the sociological model of P. Berger and T. Luckmann; studies themes of consolidation and legitimation in the historical context of "formative Judaism"; community is sectarian, competes with Galilean Pharisees, and is to be located at either Tiberias or Sepphoris. Lens is focused on Law, community, roles, and the disciples.

353 D. L. Balch (ed.). *Social History of the Matthean Community: Cross-Disciplinary Approaches.* Minneapolis: Fortress, 1991.

Four contextual themes are analyzed and debated: (1) Jewish and Hellenistic aspects; (2) women in an agrarian society; (3) Matthew and Ignatius of Antioch; (4) the social situation and location.

354 G. N. Stanton. *A Gospel for a New People: Studies in Matthew.*
Edinburgh: T. & T. Clark, 1992. Reprinted Louisville: Westmin-
ister/John Knox, 1993.
   A collection of previous articles along with eight new studies; of special importance is part two, where various angles
   are pursued to elucidate the relationship of Matthew's community to contemporary Judaism.

355 S. McKnight. "A Loyal Critic: Matthew's Polemic with Judaism
in Theological Perspective," Pp. 55–79 in *Anti-Semitism and
Early Christianity: Issues of Polemics and Faith.* Edited by C. A.
Evans and D. A. Hagner. Minneapolis: Fortress, 1993.
   Surveys Matthean theology as "intra-Jewish" polemics rather
   than anti-Semitic propaganda; Matthew debates with non-
   messianic, unbelieving Judaism. Matthew is a loyal Jew and
   the difference is hermeneutical: fulfillment in Jesus and the
   church. Israel must respond or suffer destruction.

356 D. C. Allison Jr. *The New Moses: A Matthean Typology.* Minneapolis: Fortress, 1993.
   An exhaustive analysis of the Moses "figure" in ancient
   Judaism and how Matthew's presentation of Jesus fits into
   that context. Jesus is the old and the new, the fulfillment of
   the Mosaic figure. Consequently, the faith of Matthew is also
   old and new and not just new.

357 S. C. Barton. *Discipleship and Family Ties in Mark and Matthew.*
SNTSMS 80. Cambridge: Cambridge University Press, 1994.
   The intrafamilial tension created by following Jesus is set in
   its historical context. Judaism, at its heart, provided the foundation for Jesus' call but a similar foundation can be seen in
   Greco-Roman sources; identity, so much formed in family, is
   placed in a new context by Jesus.

358 W. Carter. *Households and Discipleship: A Study of Matthew
19–20.* JSNTSS 103. Sheffield: JSOT, 1994.
   Utilizes audience-oriented criticism, historical criticism, and
   V. Turner's concept of liminality to examine Matthew 19–20
   and how it fits into Matthew's concept of discipleship. Proposes an alternative (more egalitarian) household code which
   is developed by the concept of permanent liminality (transition from one order to another).

359 U. Luz. *Matthew in History: Interpretation, Influence, and
Effects.* Minneapolis: Fortress, 1994.

Known for his "history of effects," Luz here studies how Matthew's Gospel has had various effects in the evolution of the church. Concentrates on Matthew 10 and Peter.

360 A. J. Saldarini. *Matthew's Christian-Jewish Community.* Chicago/London: University of Chicago Press, 1994.

Careful study, using historical-critical and sociological methods, of the relationship of Matthew's community to Judaism. It is a Jewish-Christian movement but not yet separated from Judaism, even if Judaism sees it as "deviant." Focuses on Israel, the leaders, the Gentiles, Law, and Christology.

361 W. R. Stegner. "Breaking Away: The Conflict with Formative Judaism." *Biblical Research* 40 (1995): 7–36.

Describes three reasons for the break of Matthew from Judaism: (1) Jesus is the final interpreter of the Law and this led Christians to be more lax; (2) Jesus was an object of worship; (3) the Jewish leaders reacted with polemic and persecution to the Christian boundary-breaking.

362 D. C. Sim. "The Gospel of Matthew and the Gentiles." *JSNT* 57 (1995): 19–48.

Counters current assumptions about the pro-Gentile orientation of Matthew; argues that Matthew's community avoided contact with Gentiles.

363 D. C. Sim. *Apocalyptic Eschatology in the Gospel of Matthew.* SNTSMS 88. New York/Cambridge: Cambridge University Press, 1996.

After carefully analyzing apocalyptic eschatology as a comprehensive worldview which focuses on the last judgment within both a dualistic and deterministic framework, Sim argues that such a view is adopted by sectarian groups under duress and this suggests a setting for the First Gospel after the Jewish War. The Gospel is a socially identifying document rather than an insensitive invective against unbelievers.

364 D. D. Kupp. *Matthew's Emmanuel: Divine Presence and God's People in the First Gospel.* SNTSMS 90. New York/Cambridge: Cambridge University Press, 1996.

Narrative analysis of a theological category: the presence of God in Matthew. Examines divine presence in the Old Testament, Matthew 1:21–23; 18:1–20; 28:16–20. Zion is no longer the center; Jesus is for Matthew.

365 Y.-E. Yang. *Jesus and the Sabbath in Matthew's Gospel.* JSNTSS 139. Sheffield: Sheffield Academic, 1997.

> Full study of Sabbath in historical context; argues that the Sabbath was a continuing issue for Matthew's community and was seen as part of Matthew's concept of fulfillment, salvation-history, and Christology.

366 J. H. Neyrey. *Honor and Shame in the Gospel of Matthew.* Louisville: Westminster/John Knox, 1998.

> Utilizes the anthropological perceptions of honor and shame in the context of ancient rhetorical genre of encomium; sees Matthew as an encomium of praise of Jesus; applies these insights to the Sermon on the Mount.

367 D. C. Sim. *The Gospel of Matthew and Christian Judaism.* SNTW. Edinburgh: T. & T. Clark, 1998.

> Argues that Matthew's community was still within Judaism, that the Gospel emerges from what is known about Antioch, and that the community is anti-Pauline.

4.2.4 Aesthetic Models of Criticism

368 J. D. Kingsbury. *Matthew: Structure: Christology, Kingdom.* Philadelphia: Fortress, 1975. New preface: 1989.

> Discipline-shaping monograph. Proposes a structural proposal that takes its shape from 4:17 and 16:21 (hence: 1:1–4:16; 4:17–16:20; 16:21–28:20) that would be developed more completely in D. R. Bauer (#371). Focuses on "titles," especially "Son of God" as the central title and christological affirmation. Salvation-history operates in two phases: (1) Israel and promise; (2) Jesus and fulfillment. The time of the church is within the time of Jesus.

369 J. D. Kingsbury. *Matthew as Story.* Philadelphia: Fortress, 1986. Second edition: 1988.

> Building on his earlier study (#368), establishes his understanding of Son of God Christology by a narrative approach; additional studies on the Son of Man (modifying his earlier study), speeches, antagonists, disciples, and the community of Matthew.

370 D. Verseput. *The Rejection of the Humble Messianic King: A Study of the Composition of Matthew 11–12.* European University Studies 291. Frankfurt am Main: Peter Lang, 1986.

Composition-critical study; Jesus and his disciples are contrasted with Jewish hostility as Jesus assumes the mantle of a humble and tender Messiah, a mission set down in the eternal purpose of God.

371 D. R. Bauer. *The Structure of Matthew's Gospel: A Study in Literary Design.* JSNTSS 31. Bible and Literature Series 15. Sheffield: Almond, 1988.

A defense of the Kingsbury structural proposal; utilizes Robert Traina's categories of literary features to argue the thesis.

372 D. J. Weaver. *Matthew's Missionary Discourse: A Literary Critical Analysis.* JSNTSS 38. Sheffield: JSOT, 1990.

Narrative analysis of Matthew 9:35–11:1, utilizing the seminal study of S. S. Lanser. Resolves the textual tension by abandoning historical explanations and seeing a narrative unity.

373 J. D. Kingsbury. "The Rhetoric of Comprehension in the Gospel of Matthew." *NTS* 41 (1995): 358–77.

Examines the "rhetoric of comprehension," or how the author presents the theme of comprehension on the part of his "characters" in his narrative framework; key factors are perception, cognition, and reaction. Correct comprehension is indicated by receiving Jesus and doing the will of God.

374 D. R. Bauer and M. A. Powell. *Treasures New and Old: Recent Contributions to Matthean Studies.* SBL Symposium Series 1. Atlanta: Scholars, 1996.

A collection of recent studies of Matthew, most of which grew out of SBL's important Matthew Group, ably directed by J. D. Kingsbury and C. Talbert. Essays are grouped into (1) composition, (2) narration, and (3) reception in light of the methodological orientations of the authors.

375 W. Carter. *Matthew: Storyteller, Interpreter, Evangelist.* Peabody, Mass.: Hendrickson, 1996.

A narrative approach to Matthew: read the Gospel as the first readers would. (1) Before reading—culture, genre, religious and social contexts; (2) reading—point of view, plot, settings, and characters; (3) after reading—comparison of authorial audience with modern readers.

5

The Gospel of Mark

As its later editor Matthew, Mark's Gospel entered the twentieth century as the historical framework for reconstructing the life of Jesus but, after the crushing blow of Wilhelm Wrede (#397) and the redactional innovations seen by Willi Marxsen (#400), Mark is now seen as a theologian with some literary flair. Although introductory issues are continually debated, in particular the date and setting of Mark's Gospel, the theological study of Mark has demonstrated his contribution especially to earliest Christianity in the arenas of Christology and discipleship. As with the other Synoptists, Mark's Gospel has been subjected to nearly every conceivable form of methodology, many of which are grouped below as "aesthetic models."

5.0 Introductory Issues (Author, Date, Purpose, Audience)

Rarely do critical scholars defend a traditional view of authorship but in the case of Mark some have suggested it as a viable alternative. Debate has raged over the date of Mark, with the destruction of Jerusalem the watershed (Hengel, #426). Study of the purpose of Mark, along with its audience, dovetails immediately into the redactional work spawned by Marxsen and others and the debate shows no sign of immediate resolution.

376 R. Martin. *Mark: Evangelist and Theologian.* Grand Rapids: Zondervan, 1972.

Comprehensive survey of redaction-critical investigations. Proposes that Mark was produced for christological motives to confirm and supplement Paul's gospel. History undergirds the Gospel and discipleship is patterned after Christology.

377 H. C. Kee. *Community of the New Age: Studies in Mark's Gospel.* Philadelphia: Westminster, 1977.

Sets the Gospel in an apocalyptic community; see #424.

378 S. P. Kealy. *Mark's Gospel: A History of Interpretation.* New York: Paulist, 1982.

A convenient listing of major studies of Mark in chronological order; ties some of strings of history together. General topics guide scholarship from Papias to Martin Hengel (#426).

379 E. Best. *Mark: The Gospel of Story.* SNTW. Edinburgh: T. & T. Clark, 1983.

A collection of essays and responses to a wide spectrum of studies and methods in Markan studies.

380 P. Pokorny. "Das Markusevangelium. Literarische und theologische Einleitung mit Forschungsbericht." Pp. 1970–2035 in *Aufstieg und Niedergang der römischen Welt.* 2.25.3. Edited by H. Temporini and W. Haase. Berlin: W. de Gruyter, 1983.

Comprehensive survey of scholarship on Mark's Gospel; surveys studies on the eschatology, the Gospel as memory, structure, Christology, and introductory matters. Emerges from early Christian preaching.

381 W. Telford (ed.). *The Interpretation of Mark.* Issues in Religion and Theology 7. London: SPCK/Philadelphia: Fortress, 1985. Second edition: Edinburgh: T. & T. Clark, 1995.

An important sifting of scholarship; influential essays by E. Schweizer, T. J. Weeden, K. Kertelge, N. Perrin, J. Dewey, E. Best, R. C. Tannehill, and S. Schulz. Second edition expands introduction and adds five articles.

382 F. J. Matera. *What Are They Saying about Mark?* Mahwah, N.J.: Paulist, 1987.

A readable survey of the history of Markan scholarship; covers themes and methodology: setting, Christology, disciples, composition, and narrative.

383 R. A. Guelich. "Mark, Gospel of." Pp. 512–25 in *Dictionary of Jesus and the Gospels*. Edited by J. B. Green, S. McKnight, and I. H. Marshall. Downers Grove, Ill.: InterVarsity, 1992.

Comprehensive survey of the main issues in Markan scholarship; utilizes a classic redaction-critical approach with a slight narrative approach; concentrates on Mark's theology (kingdom, Christology, messianic secret, and discipleship).

384 C. Bryan. *A Preface to Mark: Notes on the Gospel in its Literary and Cultural Settings*. New York: Oxford University Press, 1993.

Innovative suggestion that Mark's Gospel was designed for oral transmission and production.

385 M. M. Jacobs. "Mark's Jesus through the Eyes of Twentieth Century New Testament Scholars." *Neotestamentica* 28 (1994): 53–85.

Studies the major Christologies of Mark: messianic secret, "divine man," teacher, Son of God, and the Jesus of the Markan narrative. Emphasis today is on Jesus' humanity.

5.1 Commentaries

Recent scholarly production of commentaries on Mark is not as extensive as that of Matthew or Luke but there is nonetheless a fine history of commentaries on Mark. Modern commentaries on Mark turned over a new leaf when Vincent Taylor produced his magnificent commentary; here we find the first full engagement with the challenges of form criticism and an attempt is made to reveal pre-Markan tradition latent in the Gospel. A tragic note needs to be sounded here: perhaps the most promising commentary on Mark was in preparation when R. A. Guelich's sudden passing deprived a generation of scholars the insights that he had gathered after years of examining Mark. We are grateful for what has been published and for C. A. Evans's willingness to carry on his work.

386 V. Taylor. *The Gospel according to St. Mark*. London: Macmillan, 1952. Second edition: 1966.

An exegetical, technical commentary that interacts extensively with the rise of form criticism as enunciated by Dibelius and Bultmann. Helpful survey of Markan theology; argues for a general historical orientation to the Gospel. Noteworthy additional notes on such themes as the Twelve and the apostles, the compilation of the apocalyptic discourses, and the date of the Last Supper.

387 C. E. B. Cranfield. *The Gospel According to St. Mark.* Cambridge Greek Testament Commentary. Cambridge: Cambridge University Press, 1959.

Exegetical; critical; examines the theory that Peter stood behind Mark. Presents the Gospel as christological at its core.

388 W. Grundmann. *Das Evangelium nach Markus.* Theologischer Handkommentar zum Neuen Testament. Berlin: Evangelische Verlagsanstalt, 1959. Second edition: 1977.

Exegetical; draws upon form criticism; excellent command of the Old Testament context for Mark; author was anti-Semitic (see #301).

389 E. Schweizer. *The Good News according to Mark.* Translated by D. H. Madvig. Atlanta: John Knox, 1970. Original title: *Das Evangelium nach Markus.* NTD 1; Göttingen: Vandenhoeck & Ruprecht, 1967.

The first redaction- and composition-critical commentary; very useful for literary and theological analysis; strong on Christology and discipleship.

390 W. L. Lane. *A Commentary on the Gospel of Mark.* New International Commentary on the New Testament. Grand Rapids: Eerdmans, 1973. Second edition: 1994.

The major evangelical commentary of this century; the author provides a sketch of the history of interpretation with his own solid proposals; theologically sensitive; exegetically oriented and composition-critical in approach.

391 R. Pesch. *Das Markusevangelium.* I. Teil: *Einleitung und Kommentar zu Kap. 1,1–8,26.* II. Teil: *Kommentar zu Kap. 8,27–16,20.* Herders Theologischer Kommentar zum Neuen Testament. Freiburg: Herder, 1977.

Intensive tradition-critical study of Mark; brilliant command of details and contemporary discussion; perceptive at the redactional and theological levels.

392 J. Gnilka. *Das Evangelium nach Markus.* 1. Teilband: *Mk 1–8,26.* 2. Teilband: *Mk 8,27–16,20.* Evangelisch-Katholischer Kommentar zum Neuen Testament. Zürich: Benziger Verlag, 1979.

Thorough critical analysis; sensitive to Markan theology and composition.

393 C. S. Mann. *Mark: A New Translation with Introduction and Commentary.* Anchor Bible 27. Garden City, N.Y.: Doubleday, 1986.

Eccentric; proponent of the Griesbach Hypothesis; disappointingly, however, fails to address key source-critical questions; linguistically useful.

394 R A. Guelich. *Mark 1–8:26.* Word Biblical Commentary 34A. Dallas: Word Books, 1989.

Exhaustive tradition-critical analysis of the various layers of the Second Gospel; C. A. Evans will complete the work. Guelich's work is sensitive at all levels: critical, theological, and compositional. Christology and kingdom offer both model and hope for a beleaguered community.

395 H. Riley. *The Making of Mark: An Exploration.* Macon, Ga.: Mercer University Press, 1989.

A commentary on Mark written from the Griesbach Hypothesis viewpoint to "test whether or not this process leads to a more adequate explanation of how Mark was written" (p. x). Concludes, at the end of the commentary, that this hypothesis "stands the test" (p. 209). Mark is a reduction of Matthew and Luke; important appendixes on duality, the Last Supper, and the authorship/date of the Synoptics.

396 M. D. Hooker. *The Gospel according to Saint Mark.* Black's New Testament Commentary. London: A. & C. Black/Peabody, Mass.: Hendrickson, 1991.

A masterful study that examines the text from the angles of both history and theology.

5.2 Special Studies

The Gospel of Mark was a "life of Jesus" simply and totally—until Wilhelm Wrede (#397) suggested that Mark had fabricated the "messianic secret" and had foisted a theory of history upon what had been seen as simple history. R. H. Lightfoot, with less flair, suggested that Mark was theological thoroughly and the race was on for who could reach Mark's fundamental theological outlook first. Such a redaction-critical and theological approach to Mark, however, assumed a newer life when David Rhoads and Donald Michie (#430) proposed, first among the Synoptists, that a literary approach to the Gospel revealed an author who was doing more than writing history or theology. Just prior to this, Howard Clark Kee (#424) had adumbrated the beginnings of what is now the social-scientific perspective on Mark although fewer studies from a strictly historical or social descriptive approach have appeared in comparison to Matthew and Luke. Once again, distinguishing between "redaction/theological" studies and those of a more "historical" orientation is not easy to accomplish; I try to permit the thrust of the book to determine its classification.

5.2.1 Redaction-Critical and Theological Studies

397 W. Wrede. *The Messianic Secret*. Translated by J. C. G. Greig. Cambridge/London: James Clarke, 1971. Original title: *Das Messiasgeheimnis in den Evangelien. Zugleich ein Beitrag zum Verständnis des Markusevangeliums*. Göttingen: Vandenhoeck & Ruprecht, 1901.

When historical Jesus studies were under siege from the paradigm shift that was evoked under Johannes Weiss and Albert Schweitzer, Wrede threw down the gauntlet in front of the interpreters; he contended that Mark was fundamentally theological and unhistorical. That Jesus gave himself out to be Messiah during his life is a Markan creation; the "veil of secrecy" betrays that Jesus never thought of himself as Messiah. Examines the parable theory of Mark 4:11, the theme of silence, and the misunderstanding of the disciples.

398 R. H. Lightfoot. *The Gospel Message of St. Mark*. Oxford: Clarendon, 1950.

Anticipates the transition from form-critical to redaction-critical study.

399 G. R. Beasley-Murray. *Jesus and the Last Days: The Interpretation of the Olivet Discourse*. Peabody, Mass.: Hendrickson, 1993. Originally *Jesus and the Future: An Examination of the Criticism of the Eschatological Discourse, Mark 13; with Special Reference to the Little Apocalypse Theory*. London: Macmillan, 1954.

An exhaustive history of interpretation of Mark 13 and the Little Apocalypse Theory; includes an innovative commentary.

400 W. Marxsen. *Mark the Evangelist. Studies on the Redaction History of the Gospel*. Translated by J. Boyce, et al. Nashville: Abingdon, 1969. Original title: *Der Evangelist Markus: Studien zur Redaktionsgeschichte des Evangeliums*. Göttingen: Vandenhoeck & Ruprecht, 1956. Second edition: 1958.

Heavily influential redactional study of Mark; four independent studies (John the Baptist, geography, "gospel," and Mark 13) converge with respect to the value of redaction analysis for determining theology and setting, which the author sees involving Galilee and the parousia. The disciples are to gather there (just prior to the destruction of Jerusalem) to await the parousia.

401 J. M. Robinson. *The Problem of History in Mark and Other Marcan Studies.* Philadelphia: Fortress, 1982. Original publication: 1957.

Republication of a smaller monograph and two studies (1970, 1978). Mark wrote his Gospel by placing back on the "historical Jesus" his Easter theology and this has support in the gnostic sources. The time of Jesus is a cosmic struggle and this led to his perception of Mark as an aretalogy.

402 R. P. Meye. *Jesus and the Twelve: Discipleship and Revelation in Mark's Gospel.* Grand Rapids: Eerdmans, 1968.

Response to the use of negative dimension of the Twelve/disciples in scholarship; instead, God used the unlikely and failing disciples to establish the kingdom of God. Shows the inextricable relationship of discipleship and Christology.

403 Q. Quesnell. *The Mind of Mark: Interpretation and Method through the Exegesis of Mark 6,52.* Analecta Biblica 38. Rome: Pontifical Biblical Institute, 1969.

Examines the question of methodology (redaction criticism); uses Mark 6:52 as a test case. Sees a "eucharistic reading" of Mark 6:52 as the most probable.

404 J. R. Donahue. *Are You the Christ? The Trial Narratives in the Gospel of Mark.* SBLDS 10. Missoula: Society of Biblical Literature, 1973.

An early redaction-critical study of the trial narratives, with special focus on Mark's presentation of the temple and Christology. The two themes, anti-temple and Son of Man Christology, find their climax in the construction of a trial scene by Mark.

405 W. H. Kelber. *The Kingdom in Mark: A New Place and a New Time.* Philadelphia: Fortress, 1974.

Examines Mark through the lens of the kingdom; major antithesis is formed between Galilee and Jerusalem, with Galilee being the locus of the kingdom and Gentile Christianity maintaining priority.

406 W. H. Kelber (ed.). *The Passion in Mark: Studies on Mark 14–16.* Philadelphia: Fortress, 1976.

Collection of essays, mostly by authors having some connection to Norman Perrin, from a redaction-, composition-, and (the then beginning) literary-critical method. Consensus is that Mark did not inherit the Passion narrative and that Christology is at the center of Mark 14–16; questions the "rival" Christology theory associated with T. J. Weeden (#422).

407 H. Räisänen. *The 'Messianic Secret' in Mark.* Translated by C. Tuckett. SNTW. Edinburgh: T. & T. Clark, 1990. Updated revision of original 1976 German *Das 'Messiasgeheimnis' im Markusevangelium. Ein redaktionsgeschichtlicher Versuch.* Helsinki, 1976.

Wrede (#397) set the agenda for a century. The secrecy motif is neither the center of the Gospels nor is it a singular but rather complex motif. Further, it has been too broadly conceived by allowing "nonsecret" elements to confuse the data and resolution (e.g., parables, miracles, etc.). The issue is Christology: Jesus cannot be understood until Easter.

408 E. J. Pryke. *Redactional Style in the Marcan Gospel: A Study of Syntax and Vocabulary as Guides to Redaction in Mark.* SNTSMS 33. Cambridge: Cambridge University Press, 1978.

An examination of Mark which shows the words of Mark that are redactional and traditional.

409 E. Best. *Following Jesus: Discipleship in the Gospel of Mark.* JSNTSS 4. Sheffield: JSOT, 1981.

An intense, redaction-critical investigation of a theme in Mark. Disciples are on a journey together as they follow Jesus in the way of the cross and mission. Discipleship is seen in its individual, communal, and missional dimensions; it is also tied into Christology.

410 J. D. Kingsbury. *The Christology of Mark's Gospel.* Philadelphia: Fortress, 1983.

Jesus is the Davidic Messiah-King, but especially the Son of God is the focus when the secrecy motif is present. Son of man does not function as a title to tell us "who Jesus is"; it is a public title pointing to Jesus as the "human being," highlighting conflict and vindication.

411 C. Tuckett (ed.). *The Messianic Secret.* Issues in Religion and Theology 1. Philadelphia: Fortress/London: SPCK, 1983.

A collection of signal essays on the messianic secret, with an introductory survey of issues and their history. Some items previously untranslated.

412 E. Best. *Disciples and Discipleship: Studies in the Gospel according to Mark.* Edinburgh: T. & T. Clark, 1986.
Collection of previously published essays by a master redaction critic of Mark; displays a profound ability to get to the heart of issues.

413 J. Marcus. *The Mystery of the Kingdom of God.* SBLDS 90. Atlanta: Scholars, 1986.
Intense analysis of Mark 4 to discern the intention of Mark 4 in light an audience-oriented redaction/composition criticism. Apocalyptic, in the sense of God's power breaking in, provides the ideological context for the Gospel.

414 M. R. Mansfield. *Spirit and Gospel in Mark.* Peabody, Mass.: Hendrickson, 1987.
Utilizes an eclectic approach; discovers a more pervasive theme of Spirit and Gospel than previously recognized.

415 K. Barta. *The Gospel of Mark.* Message of Biblical Spirituality 9. Wilmington, Del.: Michael Glazier, 1988.
Series of topics in Mark pertaining to Christian spirituality: prayer, kingdom, power, healing, blindness, and discipleship. Includes questions for small groups.

416 C. C. Black. *The Disciples according to Mark: Markan Redaction in Current Debate.* JSNTSS 27. Sheffield: JSOT, 1989.
Focuses attention on the disciples in Mark in order to examine the method of redaction criticism; queries scholarship for such diverse solutions when the "same" method is being used; suggests a complete reconceptualization within a broader hermeneutical perspective.

417 T. J. Geddert. *Watchwords: Mark 13 in Markan Eschatology.* JSNTSS 26. Sheffield: Sheffield Academic, 1989.
Mark's method is to present the "secret kingdom" in veiled form. Mark 13 responds to the request for a sign by not giving one and offering a life in the face of uncertainty. Discernment and discipleship shape the life of the Christian.

418 R. T. France. *Divine Government: God's Kingship in the Gospel of Mark.* London: SPCK, 1990.

Little known but insightful volume on Mark's theology of "divine government" (preferred over "kingdom"). Mark's (too frequently neglected) presentation of this theme is studied by looking at the secrecy theme in the parables, a personal revolution, the fulfillment of future promise in the enthronement but also in progressive establishment, and the christological focus of divine government.

419   J. Marcus. *The Way of the Lord. Christological Exegesis of the Old Testament in the Gospel of Mark.* Louisville: Westminster/John Knox, 1992.

Investigation of Mark's Christology by focusing on Christology as supported by Old Testament reference; the eschatological context that responded to the destruction of Jerusalem provided Mark with an environment in which to shape his thoughts; similarities are found between Mark and Jewish exegesis.

5.2.2 Historical and Social-Scientific Studies

420   E. Trocmé. *The Formation of the Gospel according to Mark.* Translated by P. Gaughan. London: SPCK, 1975. Original title: *La Formation de l'Évangile selon Marc.* Paris, 1963.

Mark is a singular departure from the Jerusalem-based church and reflects a missionary movement. Emphasis should be given to the Passion since it a late addition; the weight is not on Christology but on discipleship.

421   M. D. Hooker. *The Son of Man in Mark: A Study of the Background of the Term "Son of Man" and its Use in St Mark's Gospel.* London: SPCK, 1967.

"Son of man" was a term for Israel as Adam's true heir. Mark uses the term to denote Jesus' rule in Israel's history: proclaimed, denied, and vindicated. He is the one on whom their fate depends (but Hooker does not see Son of man as rigorously corporate). All three dimensions of Son of man cohere in Mark's theological pattern.

422   T. J. Weeden. *Mark-Traditions in Conflict.* Philadelphia: Fortress, 1971.

Sees in Mark's Gospel a conflict of parties who differ on Christology; seen through the character of the disciples. Wonder workers *(theioi andres)* and the Suffering Servant correspond to the Twelve and Jesus. Thus, the Twelve represent false teachers in their Christology.

423 R. Martin. *Mark: Evangelist and Theologian.* Grand Rapids: Zondervan, 1972.
> Comprehensive survey of redaction-critical investigations. Proposes that Mark was produced for christological motives to confirm and supplement Paul's gospel. History undergirds the Gospel and discipleship is patterned after Christology.

424 H. C. Kee. *Community of the New Age: Studies in Mark's Gospel.* Philadelphia: Westminster, 1977.
> An innovative and discussion-shaping study of Mark that utilizes historical, literary, and sociological methods. Examines especially Christology and ecclesiology. Apocalyptic context of Mark's community is given particular emphasis as is also the charismatic context; shapes a suffering Christology.

425 M. J. Cook. *Mark's Treatment of the Jewish Leaders.* NovTestSuppl 51. Leiden: E. J. Brill, 1978.
> Historical investigation of the various titles given by Mark to Jewish leaders. Matthew and Luke depend on Mark for their "knowledge" of the leaders; Mark is an unreliable guide to the prominent figures in Judaism. Rome was not behind the death of Jesus.

426 M. Hengel. *Studies in the Gospel of Mark.* Translated by J. Bowden. Philadelphia: Fortress, 1985.
> Three technical studies of Mark as a preface to a full study of the Gospel; examines provenance, Mark as a theologian, and the titles of the Gospel of Mark. Includes excursus on Peter (R. Feldmeier), W. Schadewaldt (M. Schadewaldt), and an important study of the reliability of the Synoptic tradition (W. Schadewaldt).

427 R. P. Booth. *Jesus and the Laws of Purity: Tradition History and Legal History in Mark 7.* JSNTSS 13. Sheffield: JSOT, 1986.
> Examines the attitude of Jesus and the early Christians to the Law. Intense tradition-critical and "historico-legal criticism." Jesus denied cultic purity only in relation to ethical purity; Gentile Christians and Mark justified their freedom from the Law by appealing to Jesus; Matthew supports a traditional stance.

428 B. L. Mack. *A Myth of Innocence: Mark and Christian Origins.* Philadelphia: Fortress, 1988.

Christianity, as it has unfolded in history, is the result of Mark's "mythic" interpretation of history through his apocalyptic Gospel; situates this "myth" into intense rivalry with the synagogue; extremely skeptical and imaginative.

429 B. W. Henaut. *Oral Tradition and the Gospels: The Problem of Mark 4.* JSNTSS 82. Sheffield: JSOT, 1993.

One cannot move through the text to an oral phase; the orality of the traditions has been lost and is not accessible to those seeking the historical Jesus. Mark 4 is used as a test case.

5.2.3 Aesthetic Models of Criticism

430 D. Rhoads and D. Michie. *Mark as Story: An Introduction to the Narrative of a Gospel.* Philadelphia: Fortress, 1982. Second edition with J. Dewey: 1999.

Interdisciplinary and ground-breaking study of Mark; Rhoads is a New Testament historian and Michie an English teacher; examines rhetoric, settings, plot, and characters. Second edition revises and adds new material.

431 E. S. Malbon. *Narrative Space and Mythic Meaning in Mark.* San Francisco: Harper & Row, 1986.

Innovative, structuralist study of "space" in Mark.

432 J. D. Kingsbury. *Conflict in Mark: Jesus, Authorities, Disciples.* Minneapolis: Fortress, 1989.

Narrative approach to the major "lines" of Mark's Gospel: the stories of Jesus, the authorities, and the disciples. For Jesus, identity is tied to his destiny at the cross; the authorities possess no divine authority and are therefore blind to Jesus; the disciples, although granted a call from Jesus, remain unfaithful and at the end desert Jesus even if they are eventually reconciled.

433 R. M. Fowler. *Let the Reader Understand: Reader–Response Criticism and the Gospel of Mark.* Minneapolis: Fortress, 1991.

Reader–response method. See #234.

434 J. C. Anderson and S. D. Moore (eds.). *Mark and Method: New Approaches in Biblical Studies.* Minneapolis: Fortress, 1992.

A set of articles utilizing contemporary critical models of interpretation: narrative, reader–response, deconstruction, feminist, and social criticisms.

435 E. K. Broadhead. *Teaching with Authority: Miracles and Christology in the Gospel of Mark.* JSNTSS 74. Sheffield: JSOT, 1992.
Narrative analysis of Mark to determine the relationship of miracles and Christology. Mark utilized a variety of miracle traditions; the miracle is reoriented around the characterization of Jesus; the Christology is multifaceted but not dichotomous with the Passion.

436 J. Camery-Hoggatt. *Irony in Mark's Gospel: Text and Subtext.* SNTSMS 72. Cambridge: Cambridge University Press, 1992.
Literary analysis of "irony"; there is tension between the exclusionary strategies and the veiled revelations. This invites the reader to share the ideological point of view and to come to faith.

437 V. K. Robbins. *Jesus the Teacher: A Socio-Rhetorical Interpretation of Mark.* Minneapolis: Fortress, 1992.
A rhetorical-critical analysis that builds on the insights of composition and narrative criticism; anchors the "genre" of Mark into Jewish and Greco-Roman conventions. Analyzes how Jesus interacts with the disciples as a disciple-gathering teacher who dies for his views; three phases of teaching are discerned (1:14–3:6; 3:7–12:44; 13:1–15:47). Few studies of Mark are this broad in methodological dexterity.

438 D. H. Juel. *A Master of Surprise: Mark Interpreted.* Minneapolis: Fortress, 1994.
An introduction to Mark from a theological and rhetorical angle; chapters include studies of the baptism, parables, discipleship, and Christology.

439 H. Kinukawa. *Women and Jesus in Mark: A Japanese Feminist Perspective.* The Bible and Liberation Series. Maryknoll, N.Y.: Orbis, 1994.
Examines Mark through the lenses of rhetorical and feminist criticism; argues that women's responses led Jesus to become a "boundary breaker"; her Japanese context sheds further light on the issues.

440 E. K. Broadhead. *Prophet, Son, Messiah: Narrative Form and Function in Mark 14–16.* JSNTSS 97. Sheffield: JSOT, 1994.
Narrative analysis; focus on Christology that is multifaceted but unites prophetic and Passion themes. Text shaped by a community over an extended time; the Gospel is an exemplar and kerygma.

441 T. Shepherd. "The Narrative Function of Markan Intercalation." *NTS* 41 (1995): 522–40.

Studies the famous "intercalation" passages in Mark (3:20–35; 5:21–43; 6:7–32; 11:12–25; 14:1–11, 53–72) and proposes a resolution: the lack of a major character and separation of space, together with defocalization of the outer story as it awaits conclusion leads to a theory of "dramatized irony" for these sections in Mark.

442 D. J. Harrington. "What and Why Did Jesus Suffer according to Mark?" *Chicago Studies* 34 (1995): 32–41.

Jesus suffers and dies as part of the motif of misunderstanding and rejection; three rationales are provided in the literary presentation: (1) this was the divine plan, (2) he died for others, and (3) he is an example for those who also suffer.

443 M. I. Wegener. *Cruciformed: The Literary Impact of Mark's Story of Jesus and His Disciples.* Lanham, Md.: University Press of America, 1995.

Knowledgeable study of Mark's literary design; proceeds through the text under the thematic guideline of a "cruciformed" Christology.

444 D. Rhoads. "Mission in the Gospel of Mark." *Currents in Theology and Mission* 22 (1995): 340–55.

Utilizes a narrative approach (see #430); Mark's entire Gospel is shaped by a mission in light of the end; Mark's "community" is oriented toward mission.

445 T. Dwyer. *The Motif of Wonder in the Gospel of Mark.* JSNTSS 128. Sheffield: Sheffield Academic, 1996.

An examination of the motif in Mark using redaction and narrative criticism. Surveys the motif in Greco-Roman, Jewish, and early Christian literature; wonder is the response to divine intervention as God breaks into the world in the arrival of the kingdom.

6

The Gospel of Luke

The Gospel of Luke, partly because it was attached to Acts and thereby was distinct among early Christian writings, has enjoyed a history of scholarship that returns time and again to this two-volume work for historical, theological, and literary motives. Since the 1960s, however, the work on this Gospel has exploded and the old adage that it is a "storm center" has remained true for three decades. Along with the other Synoptic Gospels, Luke began this century as a "biography" of Jesus and went through the same metamorphosis that the others did: Luke went from biographer to theologian and literary artisan. But it was both Luke's more sophisticated Greek and his decision to extend the "history" into a second volume covering the growth of the Christian movement to Rome that gave scholars a special reason to treat the literary and theological dimensions of his work with special care. The companion volume in this series by J. B. Green and M. C. McKeever (#455) provides a more complete listing of entries.

6.0 Introductory Issues (Author, Date, Purpose)

Luke's own prefaces have led scholars to place the Gospel in a set of "popular histories" in the ancient world, but such a classification has not provided us with a consensus on any of the standard introductory issues. The authorship of Luke has been hotly disputed, with some authors continuing to argue the line that Luke was the physician companion of Paul. In spite of the ending of Acts, with Paul in prison, which was at one time a clear indicator of its date, today many see such a move as a literary artifice and that the whole corpus is more accurately dated later in the first century. As for purpose, the older idea that Luke sought to defend the legal status for the Christian religion alongside that of Judaism has given way to newer, more theological, canonical, and literary motives.

446 A. von Harnack. *Luke the Physician: The Author of the Third Gospel and the Acts of the Apostles.* New Testament Studies 1. Translated by J. R. Wilkinson. London: Williams & Norgate/ New York: Putnam, 1907.

An early defense of the traditional origins of Luke; its "feminine element" may be traced to Philip and his prophesying daughters. "Under his hands the universalistic and humane, the social and individualistic tendencies of Hellenism, the ecstatic and magical elements of Greek religion, yet also the Greek thought and sense of form, gain the mastery over the subject-matter of the traditional narratives" (p. 163).

447 C. K. Barrett. *Luke the Historian in Recent Study.* London: Epworth, 1961.

Now dated; a "state of the art" study when scholarship was turning from historical orientations to redaction criticism. Assesses the studies of Dibelius, Morgenthaler, Conzelmann, and Haenchen.

448 W. C. van Unnik. "Luke–Acts: A Storm Center in Contemporary Scholarship." Pp. 15–32 in *Studies in Luke–Acts.* Edited by L. Keck and J. L. Martyn. Nashville: Abingdon, 1966. Reprinted in W. C. van Unnik, *Sparsa Collecta: The Collected Essays of W.C. van Unnik.* Volume 1: *Evangelica—Paulina—Acta.* Pp. 92–110. NovTestSuppl 29. Leiden: E. J. Brill, 1973.

Surveys Lukan scholarship of the 1950s and 1960s when scholarship was turning to redaction criticism and leaving behind historical questions; urges a more comprehensive approach to Luke–Acts (in its historical context).

449 C. H. Talbert (ed.). *Perspectives on Luke–Acts.* Perspectives in Religious Studies; Special Studies Series 5. Danville, Va.: Association of Baptist Professors of Religion, 1978.

A selection of papers presented at the SBL Luke–Acts Group from 1972 to 1978. Introductory issues, forms, sections, and themes are discussed.

450 F. Bovon. *Luke the Theologian: Thirty-Three Years of Research (1950–1983).* Translated by K. McKinney. Pittsburgh Theological Monograph Series 12. Allison Park, Pa.: Pickwick, 1987. Original title: *Luc le Théologien. Vingt-cinq ans de Recherches (1950–75).* Second edition: Genéve: Labor et Fides, 1988.

A survey of scholarship. Includes a chronological bibliography and a discussion of the main contours. Topics: salvation-history, use of the Old Testament, Christology, Holy Spirit, salvation, reception of salvation, and the church. Now dated.

451 M. Rese. "Lukas-Evangelium: Eine Forschungsbericht." Pp. 2259–2328 in *Aufstieg und Niedergang der römischen Welt.* 2.25.3. Edited by H. Temporini and W. Haase. Berlin: W. de Gruyter, 1983.

Examines the history of Lukan scholarship in large periods (precritical, critical, 1900–1950, 1950–present); exhaustive bibliography.

452 M. A. Powell. *What Are They Saying about Luke?* New York/Mahwah: Paulist, 1989.

Lucid survey of recent study of Luke.

453 D. L. Bock. "Luke, Gospel of." Pp. 495–510 in *Dictionary of Jesus and the Gospels.* Edited by J. B. Green, S. McKnight, and I. H. Marshall. Downers Grove, Ill.: InterVarsity, 1992.

Helpful introduction to the major issues in Luke studies; covers introductory issues, structure and argument, and the theology of Luke (divine plan, Christology and salvation, new community, mission, ethics, and accountability).

454 M. C. Parsons and R. I. Pervo. *Rethinking the Unity of Luke and Acts.* Minneapolis: Fortress, 1993.

Alhough modern scholarship since Cadbury has virtually assumed the unity of Luke–Acts (note the hyphen), this assumption needs both challenge and nuance. Some senses of unity but Acts is a "sequel" to Luke: thus "Luke *and* Acts" not "Luke–Acts."

455 J. B. Green and M. C. McKeever. *Luke–Acts and New Testament Historiography.* IBR Bibliographies 8. Grand Rapids: Baker, 1994.

A full bibliography of Luke, emphasizing narrative, theology, genre, and historiography. Companion volume to this one. Topics provide a short survey of the history of interpretation.

456 C. M. Tuckett (ed.). *Luke's Literary Achievement. Collected Essays.* JSNTSS 116. Sheffield: Sheffield Academic, 1995.

A collection of essays assessing and demonstrating the variety of methods used in Lukan studies.

6.1 Commentaries

Commentaries in the first half of this century were preoccupied with the issues of source criticism raised by B. H. Streeter (#116) but, with the rise of redaction criticism, a new phase of Lukan studies began and a new zeal for the text of Luke was born. Such concerns climaxed in the two-volume commentary of J. A. Fitzmyer (#459) but those concerns quickly dissipated into the growth of aesthetic concerns: literary, rhetorical, and canonical studies that focused on the literary art and final form of Luke. The literary study of Luke now has a noteworthy example in J. B. Green (#467).

457 J. M. Creed. *The Gospel according to St. Luke.* London: Macmillan, 1930.
Early source-critical work; exegetical.

458 G. B. Caird. *The Gospel of St. Luke.* London: Penguin, 1963. Reprinted Philadelphia: Westminster, 1977.
Brief but excellent study of Luke's theological orientations; good on biblical context.

459 J. A. Fitzmyer. *The Gospel according to Luke: Introduction, Translation, and Notes.* Anchor Bible 28, 28A. 2 volumes. Garden City, N.Y.: Doubleday, 1981, 1985.
Exhaustive, form-, source-, and redaction-critical study; complete bibliographies.

460 F. W. Danker. *Jesus and the New Age: A Commentary on St. Luke's Gospel.* Philadelphia: Fortress, 1972. Revised edition: 1988.
Predecessor of literary approaches; exegetical; keenly aware of the Roman social dynamics at work behind Luke.

461 I. H. Marshall. *The Gospel of Luke. A Commentary on the Greek Text.* New International Greek Testament. Grand Rapids: Eerdmans, 1978.
Tradition- and redaction-critical study; focuses on historical accuracy of the Lukan Gospel as well as on the theological factors at work.

462 E. Schweizer. *The Good News according to Luke.* Translated by D. E. Green. Atlanta: John Knox/ London: SPCK, 1984. Original title: *Das Evangelium nach Lukas.* Göttingen: Vandenhoeck & Ruprecht, 1984.
Readable; composition-critical analysis of structure and theology.

463 R. C. Tannehill. *The Narrative Unity of Luke–Acts: A Literary Interpretation.* Volume 1: *The Gospel according to Luke.* Philadelphia: Fortress, 1986.
         Pioneering literary and rhetorical analysis; focuses on narrative roles; operates on the basis of the unity of Luke–Acts.

464 M. D. Goulder. *Luke: A New Paradigm.* JSNTSS 20. Sheffield: JSOT, 1989.
         Argues that Luke did not use Q but only Mark and Matthew in his composition; the rest is Lukan redaction and creation. Imaginative scholar.

465 J. Nolland. *Luke.* Word Biblical Commentary 35A, B, C. 3 volumes. Dallas: Word Books, 1989, 1993.
         Eclectic methodology combining redaction, composition, and historical criticism; aware of historical context; complete bibliographies.

466 D. L. Bock. *Luke.* Volume 1: *1:1–9:50.* Volume 2: *9:51–24:53.* Baker Exegetical Commentary on the New Testament 3A, 3B. Grand Rapids: Baker, 1994, 1996.
         Eclectic methodology: historical, source-, redaction-, and composition-critical study. Strong on historical accuracy of the Lukan Gospel; emphasizes the theology of Luke; also useful for homiletics.

467 J. B. Green. *The Gospel of Luke.* New International Commentary on the New Testament. Grand Rapids: Eerdmans, 1997.
         Exceptionally lucid commentary focusing on the literary and rhetorical art; sensitive to Lukan theology and social context; master of contemporary bibliography. In literary fashion, eschews introductory and historical issues (see pp. 14–20, where the author defends his approach).

6.2 Special Studies

Pride of place in the history of Lukan studies goes to the many who have grappled with Luke as a historian (see Green and McKeever, #455) even though the tide turned with the rise of redaction criticism and the development of interdisciplinary studies (called here "aesthetic criticisms"). The decision so typical of current literary approaches to the Synoptics—to avoid historical questions and to bracket issues about context—only forces the question of genre to be raised. Is Luke referential, or is it simply literary and theological? A resolution to the question of genre awaits further research. Historiographical studies have shifted more to the Acts side of the ledger but the rise of the social-scientific approach will shift some research into the historical nature of the Gospel (see Neyrey, #475; Sterling, #476). On the other hand, study of the theology of Luke has significant overlaps with much that is done from an aesthetic, especially literary, viewpoint (see Green, #499). The preponderance of entries here examine Luke from the angle of theology.

6.2.1 Historical and Social-Scientific Studies

468 W. K. Hobart. *The Medical Language of St. Luke.* Dublin: Hodges, Figgis & Co., 1882. Reprinted Grand Rapids: Baker, 1954.
Classic study of the medical terms in Luke that support a traditional authorship; the concentration of medical terms remains a fact although few today embrace the physician's authorship.

469 W. M. Ramsay. *Was Christ Born at Bethlehem? A Study on the Credibility of St. Luke.* London: Hodder & Stoughton, 1898. Reprinted Grand Rapids: Baker, 1979.
Apologetic defense of the credibility of Luke's historical details concerning the Roman enrollment. On Ramsay, see S. McKnight. "Sir William M. Ramsay." Pp. 304–7. In *More Than Conquerors.* Edited by J. Woodbridge; Chicago: Moody, 1992.

470 W. C. van Unnik. "Luke–Acts: A Storm Center in Contemporary Scholarship." Pp. 15–32 in *Studies in Luke–Acts.* Edited by L. Keck and J. L. Martyn. Nashville: Abingdon, 1966. Reprinted in W. C. van Unnik, *Sparsa Collecta: The Collected Essays of W.C. van Unnik.* Volume 1: *Evangelica—Paulina—Acta.* Pp. 92–110. NovTestSup 29. Leiden: E. J. Brill, 1973.
Surveys Lukan scholarship of the 1950s and 1960s when scholarship was turning to redaction criticism and leaving behind historical questions; urges a more comprehensive approach to Luke–Acts (in its historical context).

471 J. Drury. *Tradition and Design in Luke's Gospel: A Study in Early Christian Historiography.* Atlanta: John Knox, 1976.
Studies the historiography of Luke by examining his midrashic use of sources: Old Testament, Mark, and Matthew (following M. D. Goulder, #464). Lukan historiography shows how Christianity is the reappropriation of tradition and Luke does this in a context of secular realism.

472 P. F. Esler. *Community and Gospel in Luke–Acts: The Social and Political Motivations of Lucan Theology.* SNTSMS 57. Cambridge: Cambridge University Press, 1987.

Rather than operating from a theologically oriented ideology, Luke's theology emerges from responses to social and political factors. Utilizes a "socio-redaction criticism." Luke springs from interacting with religious diversity and economic stratification; the Christian community, as a result of its revision of Christian history, finds its identity.

473 J. T. Sanders. *The Jews in Luke–Acts.* Philadelphia: Fortress, 1987.

Luke–Acts polemicizes against the Jews in acerbic tones: "all Jews are equally, in principle at least, perverse" (p. 317). See the important responses: D. L. Tiede, in *Anti-Semitism and Early Christianity.* Edited by D. A. Hagner and C. A. Evans. Minneapolis: Fortress, 1983. Pp. 102–12; C. A. Evans, *Reimaging the Death of the Lukan Jesus.* BBB 73. Edited by D. D. Sylva. Frankfurt a. M.: A. Hain, 1990. Pp. 29–56, 174–83.

474 C. J. Thornton. *Der Zeuge des Zeugen: Lukas als Historiker der Paulusreisen.* WUNT 56. Tübingen: J. C. B. Mohr (Paul Siebeck), 1991.

Examines Luke as a companion of Paul; discusses especially the "we" passages of Acts as literary and historical phenomena; argues Luke was a companion of Paul but interpreted the events of Paul's life in light of his own theology.

475 J. H. Neyrey (ed.). *The Social World of Luke–Acts: Models for Interpretation.* Peabody, Mass.: Hendrickson, 1991.

An important collection of essays which broaden the historical-critical method of Luke–Acts to include sociological models and perspectives; especially indebted to Mary Douglass through B. J. Malina and J. Neyrey. Topics include honor and shame, labeling and deviance theories, urban social relations, healing, symbolic universe, and ceremonies.

476 G. E. Sterling. *Historiography and Self-Definition: Josephos, Luke–Acts and Apologetic Historiography.* NovTestSuppl 64. Leiden: E. J. Brill, 1992.

Luke fits into the attempts of others in the Mediterranean who rewrote the history of a people in a Hellenized form; the "lack of antiquity" is overcome by appeal to continuity with ancient Israel.

477 L. Alexander. *The Preface to Luke's Gospel: Literary Conventions and Social Context in Luke 1.1–4 and Acts 1.1.* SNTSMS 78. Cambridge: Cambridge University Press, 1993.

The background to Luke's two prefaces is investigated; they are closest to Greek scientific and technical manuals rather than technical histories; language fits the tradition that the author was a doctor.

478 H. Moxnes. "The Social Context of Luke's Community." *Interpretation* 48 (1994): 379–89.

Distinctive use of literary tools to discern the social makeup of Luke's community: urban, eastern Mediterranean, primarily nonelite mixture of ethnic groups and cultural relations.

479 S. McKnight and M. C. Williams. "Luke." Pp. 39–57 in *Historians of the Christian Tradition: Their Methodology and Influence on Western Thought.* Edited by M. Bauman and M. I. Klauber. Nashville: Broadman & Holman, 1996.

Surveys Luke's historiography; defends the essential reliability of Luke as an ancient historian.

6.2.2 Redaction-Critical and Theological Studies

480 H. Conzelmann. *The Theology of St. Luke.* Translated by G. Buswell. New York: Harper & Row, 1960. Reprinted Philadelphia: Fortress, 1982. Original title: *Die Mitte der Zeit.* Tübingen: J. C. B. Mohr (Paul Siebeck), 1953. Second edition: 1957.

The formative redaction-critical study of Luke; focuses on geography, eschatology, salvation-history, and the church. Finds three periods in salvation-history: Israel, Jesus, church. Concern has its origin in the issue of the delay of parousia and the works of O. Cullmann and R. Bultmann. Influenced studies of salvation-history in Matthew especially.

481 L. E. Keck and J. L. Martyn (eds.). *Studies in Luke–Acts.* Nashville: Abingdon, 1966. Reprinted Philadelphia: Fortress, 1980.

Influential collection of essays by noteworthy scholars; sums up the tendencies of early redaction-critics and sets Luke–Acts in its early Christian (historical) context. Studies by van Unnik, Cadbury, Minear, Dahl, and Conzelmann.

482 H. Flender. *St Luke: Theologian of Redemptive History.* Translated by R. H. Fuller and I. Fuller. Philadelphia: Fortress/London:

SPCK, 1967. Translation of author's thesis: *Heil und Geschichte in der Theologie des Lukas.*

Early response to Conzelmann's theory of salvation-history (#480); sees salvation-history as both linear and vertical. Salvation can thus be both past event and present manifestation. Utilizes some early narrative techniques; Luke combines Paul and John.

483 S. Brown. *Apostasy and Perseverance in the Theology of Luke.* Analecta Biblica 36. Rome: Pontifical Biblical Institute, 1969.

Counters individualism and Conzelmann's (#480) theory of the temptation of Jesus; "faith" is resident in the community; therefore, apostasy and perseverance are ecclesial and not individual categories; Christians are to remain in "the faith." Faith is mediated through the historical reality of the Church.

484 I. H. Marshall. *Luke: Historian and Theologian.* Grand Rapids: Zondervan, 1970. Reprinted Downers Grove, Ill.: InterVarsity, 1998.

Broad coverage of the history of redaction criticism of Luke's Gospel; proposes the concept of salvation as the center of Lukan theology; revised edition updates the discussion.

485 E. E. Ellis. *Eschatology in Luke.* Facet Books. Biblical Series 30. Philadelphia: Fortress, 1972.

Response to both Conzelmann (#480) and Flender (#482); Luke sees only two stages in eschatology: present and future. Later study of the same topic: see "Eschatology in Luke Revisited." Pp. 296–303 in *L'Évangile de Luc—The Gospel of Luke.* Revised edition. BETL 32. Leuven: Leuven University Press, 1989.

486 E. Franklin. *Christ the Lord: A Study in the Purpose and Theology of Luke–Acts.* London: SPCK, 1975.

Redaction criticism approach. Holds that Luke was written by someone who may well have been a companion of Paul; challenges current scholarship which denies the importance of eschatology to Luke; shows that even Christology is guided by eschatology. Does not reject the Jewish people but does include Gentiles as fulfillment of Old Testament promise.

487 R. Maddox. *The Purpose of Luke–Acts.* SNTW. Edinburgh: T. & T. Clark, 1982.

By investigating the themes Luke used as points of emphasis, it is concluded that the purpose is to provide confidence to a Gentile church that salvation is a present reality; they can therefore carry out the mission of the church in the face of persecution.

488 S. G. Wilson. *Luke and the Law.* SNTSMS 50. Cambridge: Cambridge University Press, 1983.

Luke's attitude toward the Law is consistently positive; negative ones need to be inferred. Zeal for the Law is a feature of the Jewish Christian while a more lenient attitude is found among Gentile Christians. See the reaction of C. L. Blomberg, *JSNT* 22 (1984): 53–80.

489 D. L. Bock. *Proclamation from Prophecy and Pattern: Lucan Old Testament Christology.* JSNTSS 12. Sheffield: JSOT, 1987.

An examination of the use of the Old Testament in Luke and Acts 1–13 to see if it is a "proof from prophecy" scheme. Instead, the author sees a proclamation of Christology on the basis of Old Testament prophecy and patterns. Focus is on the Lordship of Jesus as the climax of the Messiah-Servant role.

490 J. A. Fitzmyer. *Luke the Theologian: Aspects of His Teaching.* New York: Paulist, 1989.

Synthesis of eight discussions in Lukan theology: authorship, infancy narratives, Mary, John the Baptist, discipleship, Satan, the Law, and the death of Jesus.

491 D. P. Moessner. *Lord of the Banquet: The Literary and Theological Significance of the Lukan Travel Narrative.* Minneapolis: Fortress, 1989.

Argues for the Deuteronomic Prophet basis for Luke 9:51–19:44; sees the key to understanding this section in the motif of table fellowship; Jesus brings to fulfillment the promises to Israel and sets out a paradigm for the extension of the message to the world.

492 D. J. Ireland. *Stewardship and the Kingdom of God: An Historical, Exegetical, and Contextual Study of the Parable of the Unjust Steward in Luke 16:1–13.* NovTestSuppl 70. Leiden: E. J. Brill, 1992.

Thorough analysis of a hotly disputed parable. Utilizing the steward's "wisdom," he sees the parable as teaching faithful stewardship of one's material possessions in a context of eschatological fulfillment and expectation as well as a theology of riches and poverty.

493 C. A. Evans and J. A. Sanders. *Luke and Scripture: The Function of Sacred Tradition in Luke–Acts.* Minneapolis: Fortress, 1993.

Collection of essays, some previously published; each exemplifies the method of reappropriation of Jewish tradition for elucidating the Lukan text and its theology; the "rewritten Bible" is the use of Jesus traditions for Luke.

494 E. Scheffler. *Suffering in Luke's Gospel.* Abhandlungen zur Theologie des Alten und Neuen Testaments 81. Zürich: Theologischer Verlag, 1993.

An embracive view of suffering in Luke; themes involved in the topic: economic, social, political, physical, psychological, and spiritual. Jesus' suffering fits into the overall theme.

495 W. H. Shepherd. *The Narrative Function of the Holy Spirit as a Character in Luke–Acts.* SBLDS 147. Atlanta: Scholars, 1994.

Examines the role of the Holy Spirit as a character in Luke–Acts by exegeting through a literary lens the primary passages; sees the Holy Spirit as indirect characterization of God.

496 T. K. Seim. *The Double Message: Patterns of Gender in Luke–Acts.* Nashville: Abingdon, 1994.

Redaction-critical study of whether women are presented positively or negatively: Luke's program is double in that sometimes women are presented positively and at other times negatively.

497 J. A. Weatherly. *Jewish Responsibility for the Death of Jesus in Luke–Acts.* JSNTSS 106. Sheffield: Sheffield Academic Press, 1994.

Thorough tradition-critical analysis that argues Luke–Acts lays responsibility for the death of Jesus only on the shoulders of the leaders and people of Jerusalem.

498 M. L. Strauss. *The Davidic Messiah in Luke–Acts. The Promise and its Fulfillment in Lukan Christology.* JSNTSS 110. Sheffield: Sheffield Academic Press, 1995.

Thorough analysis of Jesus the Davidic King in the context of Jewish expectation and as understood in early Christian thinking. Shows an extensive connection to Isaiah's depiction of redemption, where one finds a prophet, servant, and king in one image.

499 J. B. Green. *The Theology of the Gospel of Luke.* New Testament Theology. Cambridge: Cambridge University Press, 1995.

A concise summary of Luke's theology in light of rhetorical, literary, and social context readings. Follows the path charted out by Marshall (#484) with respect to the centrality of salvation ("plan of God") for Lukan theology; surveys Christology, mission and salvation, discipleship, and the church. Nicely introduces his large commentary (#467).

500 H. D. Buckwalter. *The Character and Purpose of Luke's Chris-tology.* SNTSMS 89. Cambridge: Cambridge University Press, 1996.

> Examines how Luke's motives reveal his Christology: studies the purpose of Luke–Acts, how Luke handles Mark, the lord-ship of Jesus, and his emphasis on the theme of humiliation. Argues for a discipleship-exemplary form in Christology.

501 B. E. Reid. *Choosing the Better Part? Women in the Gospel of Luke.* Collegeville, Minn.: Liturgical, 1996.

> A complete exposition of women in Luke and how they par-ticipate in the call to follow Jesus in discipleship; both good and bad implications are noted.

502 P. Doble. *The Paradox of Salvation: Luke's Theology of the Cross.* SNTSMS 87. Cambridge: Cambridge University Press, 1996.

> Contests the current trend to minimize the cross in Lukan theology; the theology of the cross in Luke is coherent. Anchoring the study in Wisdom, the author argues that cross formed a paradox with resurrection to compel discipleship.

503 J. M. Arlandson. *Women, Class, and Society in Early Christian-ity: Models from Luke–Acts.* Peabody, Mass.: Hendrickson, 1997.

> Examines the place of women in Greco-Roman world, shows how Luke fits into that world; women of lower classes are ele-vated when they confront the kingdom of God, even at the expense of men.

6.2.3 Aesthetic Models of Criticism

504 C. H. Talbert. *Literary Patterns, Theological Themes, and the Genre of Luke–Acts.* SBLMS 20. Missoula: Scholars, 1974.

> Methodologically focused on "architecture analysis," a con-cern with formal patterns of Luke–Acts in the context of the whole work. Luke's work needs to be understood both liter-arily and pastorally. Applied to salvation-history, Christology, and genre (biographical succession narrative).

505 K. E. Bailey. *Poet and Peasant.* Grand Rapids: Eerdmans, 1976. *Through Peasant Eyes: A Literary-Cultural Approach to the Parables in Luke.* Grand Rapids: Eerdmans, 1980. Combined edition: 1983.

> Eclectic method shifting from historical to the literary; aware of the social conditions of the Middle East; innova-

tive in perception of structure and cultural context of Luke's
parables.

506 L. T. Johnson. *The Literary Function of Possessions in Luke–Acts.*
SBLDS 39. Missoula: Scholars, 1977.
The leaders (Moses, Jesus, apostles) are typed as "Prophet"
and those who accept their proclamation as the "People"
(emphasizing continuity). The theme of possessions functions
symbolically: to express "the inner response of men's hearts
to God's Visitation and authority" (p. 170).

507 J. M. Dawsey. *The Lukan Voice: Confusion and Irony in the
Gospel of Luke.* Macon, Ga.: Mercer University Press, 1986.
In Luke the reader is in dialogue with both the "narrator" and
the "characters"; salvation becomes real for its readers through
irony.

508 J. D. Kingsbury. *Conflict in Luke: Jesus, Authorities, Disciples.*
Minneapolis: Fortress, 1991.
Following on his similar study in Mark (#432), the author studies here Jesus, the Jewish authorities, and the disciples in the
context of conflict. Jesus is the Messiah and Son of God in
whom God inaugurates salvation; the authorities are the self-
righteous opponents of Jesus; the disciples are loyal but spiritually immature followers of Jesus.

509 K. E. Bailey. *Finding the Lost: Cultural Keys to Luke 15.* St. Louis:
Concordia, 1992.
A final treatment by one who has a "love affair" (p. 9) with the
parables of Luke 15; uses rhetorical criticism in light of a social
awareness; argues Luke 15 may be understood as an expansion
of Psalm 23 (thirteen themes are found to be connected).

510 M. C. Parsons and R. I. Pervo. *Rethinking the Unity of Luke and
Acts.* Minneapolis: Fortress, 1993.
Although modern scholarship since Cadbury has virtually
assumed the unity of Luke–Acts (note the hyphen), this
assumption needs both challenge and nuance. Some senses of
unity but Acts is a "sequel" to Luke: thus "Luke *and* Acts"
not "Luke–Acts." Challenges the entire assumption of many
of the "literary" and "canonical" studies of Luke.

511 W. S. Kurz. *Reading Luke–Acts: Dynamics of Biblical Narrative.*
Louisville: Westminster/John Knox, 1993.
Narrative and canonical approach, utilizing the lenses of
implied authors and readers; applied to Luke–Acts.

512 W. Braun. *Feasting and Social Rhetoric in Luke 14.* SNTSMS 85. Cambridge: Cambridge University Press, 1995.

Argues Luke 14:1–24 is an artistically and rhetorically arranged presentation of the ideal Christian society to the urban elites of the Lukan audience. Orders the text as: (1) Jesus heals craving desires (14:1–6), (2) rules are presented for the new symposium (14:7–14), and (3) the dinner (14:15–24).

7

Theology

Here we comment on those studies that summarize the theology of the Synoptics in a synthetic manner. We have also included single commentaries that cover all three Synoptic Gospels. Older studies, particularly those written before the rise of form and redaction criticism, under the assumption that John was not "historically useful," often assumed that the theology of the Synoptists was at the same time roughly the same as the "theology of Jesus." For this reason, we have also included some treatments where such a confusion is apparent. This distinction between the historical Jesus and the theology of the Synoptists is perhaps the most enduring methodological achievement of the twentieth century when it pertains to the critical study of the Gospels. It was Albert Schweitzer who popularized the growing consensus that one must choose either the Synoptics or John when one decides to study the teachings of Jesus. History has proved both the distinction and that most have chosen the former.

513 C. G. Montefiore. *The Synoptic Gospels.* 2 volumes. London: Macmillan, 1909. Reprinted New York: KTAV, 1968.

A precursor to the modern preoccupation with the Jewish context for Jesus and the Synoptics; includes commentaries on the Synoptics and essays of a historical and theological nature. I. Abrahams has an influential essay on the "people of the land."

514 R. Bultmann. *Theology of the New Testament.* Translated by K. Grobel. Volume 1. New York: Scribner's, 1951, 1955. Original title: *Theologie des Neuen Testaments.* Tübingen: J. C. B. Mohr (Paul Siebeck), 1948, 1953.

The most influential New Testament theology of the twentieth century. Jesus' own message is a presupposition of New Testament theology rather than part of it; the theology of the Synoptists is found in his study of the theology of the early churches. His *History of the Synoptic Tradition* (#66) and this *Theology* anticipate the later work of redactional theology.

515 C. K. Barrett. *The Holy Spirit and the Gospel Tradition.* London: SPCK, 1947. Second edition: 1966.

Technical and scholarly; more emphasis is given to the historical Jesus than to the Synoptics; examines the tension between the earliest churches and Jesus over the issue of the Holy Spirit.

516 H. Conzelmann. *Grundriß der Theologie des Neuen Testaments.* Fourth edition. Edited by A. Lindemann. Tübingen: J. C. B. Mohr, 1987. English translation of the second German edition by J. Bowden. *An Outline of the Theology of the New Testament.* New York: Harper & Row, 1969.

Delineates the various theologies of the Synoptics in typical categories (Fourth German edition only); the English translation synthesizes the three into one "theology."

517 W. G. Kümmel. *The Theology of the New Testament according to its Major Witnesses: Jesus-Paul-John.* Translated by J. E. Steely. Nashville: Abingdon, 1973. Original title: *Die Theologie des Neuen Testaments.* NTD Ergänzungsreihe 3. Göttingen: Vandenhoeck & Ruprecht, 1969.

Synthesizes the Synoptics by themes (kingdom, God, ethics, Jesus' personal claims, and his suffering and death). Under the influence of Martin Kähler's forceful argument for the church's kerygma (as opposed to a reconstructed historical Jesus), the author treats the topics as part of that kerygma.

518 G. E. Ladd. *A Theology of the New Testament.* Grand Rapids: Eerdmans, 1974. Revised edition: 1993, edited by D. A. Hagner.

Salvation-historical approach to New Testament theology that was originally conducted by examination of the Synoptic presentation of the kingdom of God. Jesus and the Synoptics are here nearly identical; an added chapter by R. T. France delineates the distinctive theologies of the Synoptists.

519 L. Goppelt. *Theology of the New Testament.* Volume 1: *The Ministry of Jesus in Its Theological Significance.* Translated by J. E. Alsup. Edited by J. Roloff. Grand Rapids: Eerdmans, 1981. Original title: *Theologie des Neuen Testaments.* Göttingen: Vandenhoeck & Ruprecht, 1975.

> An important examination of the teachings of Jesus, largely on the basis of the Synoptics; the Synoptists are then set into his unfolding of theology in the early churches. Matthew is examined with James (Syria); Luke with Hebrews (Rome); Mark is not given separate treatment.

520 R. Banks. *Jesus and the Law in the Synoptic Tradition.* SNTSMS 28. Cambridge: Cambridge University Press, 1975.

> Brilliant analysis of Jesus and the Law. Banks concludes that Jesus saw the entire Old Testament as finding its apex in his teachings and person. This book has justifiably influenced studies of Jesus' relationship to the Law, as well as how Christians read the Old Testament. The Synoptists shape their view of the Law through their respective Christologies.

521 R. E. Brown. *The Birth of the Messiah: A Commentary on the Infancy Narratives in the Gospels of Matthew and Luke.* Anchor Bible Reference Library. New York: Doubleday, 1977. Revised edition: 1993.

> Exhaustive commentary on the infancy narratives; eclectic methodology proceeding through form-, tradition-, redaction, and historical criticism. Complete bibliographies; important appendixes on Levirate marriage, virginal conception, the charge of illegitimacy, the census under Quirinius, and midrash; the second edition includes a supplement that updates scholarship.

522 J. Piper. *'Love Your Enemies.' Jesus' Love Command in the Synoptic Gospels and in the Early Christian Paraenesis.* SNTSMS 38. Cambridge: Cambridge University Press, 1979.

> A tradition-critical examination of the command to love; moves from Jesus to the early Christian paraenesis, including the historical background. Sees the demand as rooted in the enablement of God in the presence of the kingdom. Special attention given to both Matthew and Luke.

523 W. Schrage. *The Ethics of the New Testament.* Translated by D. E. Green. Philadelphia: Fortress, 1988. Original title: *Ethik des Neuen Testaments.* Göttingen: Vandenhoeck & Ruprecht, 1982.

Bucks the trend of German scholarship; begins a "New Testament theology of ethics" with the historical Jesus; highlights the redactional contours of the Synoptists.

524 R. E. Brown. *The Death of the Messiah: From Gethsemane to the Grave. A Commentary on the Passion Narratives in the Four Gospels.* 2 volumes. Anchor Bible Reference Library. New York: Doubleday, 1994.

Exhaustive analysis using an eclectic, critical method, as the author seeks to find the intention of the authors as they made those known in their narratives (see 1.4–35). Procedure "harmonizes" the texts by event in the life of Jesus. Complete bibliographies with appendixes on *The Gospel of Peter*, dating the crucifixion, Judas, sacrifice of Isaac, the Old Testament background, Jesus' predictions, and a pre-Marcan passion narrative (M. Soards).

525 G. Strecker. *Theologie des Neuen Testaments.* Edited by F. W. Horn. Berlin: W. de Gruyter, 1995.

Begins with Paul; complete study of the tradition-critical development of New Testament theology. Three fundamental issues shape Synoptic theology: (1) redactional reshapings, (2) the delay of the parousia, (3) the concept of "Gospel." Mark: messianic secret; Matthew: the way of righteousness; Luke: middle of time. Reflects German categories of early redaction criticism.

526 R. Schnackenburg. *Jesus in the Gospels: A Biblical Christology.* Translated by O. C. Dean Jr.. Louisville: Westminster/John Knox, 1995.

A comprehensive and nuanced survey of the Christology of each of Gospels. Mark: Jesus' activity and titles; Matthew: story of Jesus and his picture; Luke: the basic view and individual features. Reflections on a "four forms" as a manifold yet unified testimony to Jesus Christ.

527 J. Gibson. *The Temptations of Jesus in Early Christianity.* JSNTSS 112. Sheffield: Sheffield Academic, 1995.

An examination of the temptations traditions, especially in Mark and Q, to see the nature and content of the temptations. Fundamental unity in early Christian perception of temptations; Jesus' mission was how Israel was to be the true people of God.

528 R. B. Hays. *The Moral Vision of the New Testament: A Contemporary Introduction to New Testament Ethics. Community, Cross, New Creation.* San Francisco: HarperSanFrancisco, 1996.
A majestic sweep of important New Testament ethical themes, with pastoral implications (pp. 3–7). Mark: taking up the cross; Matthew: training for the kingdom; Luke–Acts: liberation through the power of the Spirit. An excursus covers the role of the historical Jesus in New Testament ethics.

Author Index